PRAISE FOR THE EDUCULTURE COOKBOOK

This book is one of a kind and I know it's going to make a positive impact with whoever reads it! *The EduCulture Cookbook* definitely cooks up some awesome ideas for educators to implement in their classrooms and schools. Mike is the epitome of leading by example and everything that he writes about, he's done in his own school and his culture is a testament to this awesome book!

— ADAM WELCOME - PRINCIPAL, AUTHOR, SPEAKER, PODCASTER

There is a time in every educator's life when they want to create something special at their school site and just can't get the recipe right. This was the case, until now! In this book Earnshaw lists the ingredients needed and gives you step-by-step directions to make some amazing things happen on your site.

— RYAN SHEEHY - EDUCATOR, LEAD LEARNER, AUTHOR, SPEAKER

In *The EduCulture Cookbook*, Michael Earnshaw dishes up the perfect blend of personal stories, inspiring thoughts, and creative recipes you can use in your classroom, school, or district. With his unique style, love of the culinary arts, and years of experience, Mike has created a cookbook that will keep you entertained, inspired, and excited to "taste test" a new idea every day!

— JEFF GARGAS - COO / CO-FOUNDER, TEACH BETTER TEAM, CO-AUTHOR, *TEACH BETTER*

Mike Earnshaw shares his unique stories, experiences, and inspiration to try new recipes, new ideas, new techniques in your building, classroom, or community at large. Breathe new life into your practices with Mike at your side in *The EduCulture Cookbook*, today!

— Becky Schnekser - Teacher & Author

I am not a cook, at least not a very good one. I don't know the difference between oregano and basil. I have no idea how to bake and can barely even set the clock on my microwave. What I do know, though, is that if I can follow directions, read a recipe, and add a little creativity, I can take my basic skills and turn them into a magical feast.

In this amazing book, Mike Earnshaw allows all of us to feel as though we can cook up amazing cultures and climates within our schools and classrooms. Whether you are used to standing on your head, skateboarding down the halls, or sitting behind your desk, Mike provides step by step recipes for transforming what has been brewing into a feast that all kids will want to devour. I encourage you to sit back, dive in, and begin planning for an EduCulture transformation.

— Dr. Dave Schmittou - Director of Leadership & Development Teach Better Team

Strong Culture Construction is the most important tool educators can have in their toolbox. All educators participating in a school's ecosystem carry a responsibility to continue to elevate their skills and foster reflection to enhance the learning environment of our buildings. What better way to go about this process with *The EduCulture Cookbook*?! Mike has crafted a go-to guide dedicated to ensuring the culture in our schools continues to be full of a fun, family atmosphere. We can be Better. Thank you Mike for challenging our thinking and helping us reach more students!

— Rae Hughart - CMO Teach Better Team, Teacher, Author

Mike Earnshaw delivers a five-star service with his book *The EduCulture Cookbook*. These recipes provide all educators, no matter their ability level, the strategies needed to cook up something good to enhance the ambiance and culture of their schools. Mike's humor and quick wit will keep you on your toes, but his messages are deep and they are followed up by real-life examples that will leave you inspired. This book is a must-read for all educators who want to improve their practice and ultimately contribute to an outstanding school culture.

— Robert Breyer - Principal, Podcaster, Author

Finally a book that you can read and implement ideas immediately! This book has fun practical ways to build a great culture in your school!

— Raymond Porten - Principal

This book combines a positive mindset, academia, and evidence-based practice from someone in the field doing this leadership work. Mike nailed it. I have not read an educational book written in a "cookbook" style, but I am glad I did. This book is filled with practical wisdom to create a compassionate classroom model. The tie-in to resources is marvelous and makes the book a recipe for success. A teacher is not something you do; it's who you are. With that in mind, it makes sense also to believe that there can be a manual, a how-to, a collection of suggestions designed to help teachers evolve. This book is a treasure trove of ideas to help teachers create a genuinely compassionate classroom environment. I can't recommend this book highly enough. The format makes for an easy, fun read. The recipes are clear, and the observations presented validate every word Mike has written. He has shared his experience and wisdom with us. Chock full of solid tips, excellent practices, practical applications mixed with great personal stories, and easy activities to implement, that can change any classroom environment for the better!

— Dr. Matthew X. Joseph - District Leader and Author

After consuming and digesting *The EduCulture Cookbook's* contents you will be left full and satisfied! This comprehensive guide is full of inspiration, easy to implement strategies, and motivational stories that can energize and reinvigorate the culture of any school or district! Mike Earnshaw artfully crafts not only the recipes for success but provides supporting anecdotes, testimonials, and real world application to help any leader thrive and improve their school culture!

— Chad Ostrowski - CEO & Co-founder Teach Better Team

Creative, clever, and a catalyst for betterment - *The EduCulture Cookbook* is a collection of five star recipes for building school culture. Throughout the entire book, Earnshaw's storytelling genius reveals itself through the stories of culture building examples that help you visualize and feel the emotions as if you were there. Just like an Executive Chef, Earnshaw masterfully lays out his experiences on a plate for us to taste, savor, and enjoy. This innovative cookbook is a powerfully interwoven manifesto that integrates Earnshaw's passions for skateboarding, cooking, culture, and leadership. A must read for all educators and leaders!

— Livia Chan - Head Teacher, Author, & Digital Content Editor for Teach Better Team

Culture is the *glue* that keeps everything intact in your classroom or the entire school. We all know the saying, "culture eats strategy for breakfast," and it is imperative educators understand that the culture of classrooms and schools directly impacts student achievement. *The EduCulture Cookbook* provides readers with unique and innovative "recipes" that will increase your visibility and *relationship-building* skills as an educator. In order for educators to be true agents of change, we must be comfortable with disrupting the status quo and fostering authentic equitable environments for all students to thrive. Each chapter includes real vignettes from the author and other amazing educators, as well as practical and realistic takeaways that every educator can benefit from. If you are looking for a book that will rekindle/rejuvenate your passion for building strong school cultures of change. This book is for you and you will be a better educator for it!

— Dr. Basil Marin - HS Assistant Principal/DEI Consultant

In *The EduCulture Cookbook*, Michael Earnshaw has whipped up a batch of great recipes you can use to connect with your staff, students, and community. As an educational leader he is all about building those relationships and connections and he's sharing some of that home cooked goodness with you in this book. These recipes will get your campus connections and collaboration rising. So break out your chef's hat and be ready to get cooking for a better culture on your campus!

— JOSHUA BUCKLEY - TITLE I SPECIALIST & CO-HOST OF THE PUNK ROCK CLASSROOMS PODCAST

What I am most impressed with in Mike Earnshaw's cookbook, is that the recipes here don't need to be followed to the exact ingredient. They are all able to be modified to your taste - and in the case of those who will be reading this book, that means to the taste of your students and staff. Earnshaw brings his actual experience as a Head Line Cook to the pages in *The EduCulture Cookbook*. You can sense his kitchen expertise within the pages, as he compares great recipes to great teaching and learning. They are both experiences to be savored, and the EduChef doesn't let you down.

Consider the following quote from the very first recipe in *The EduCulture Cookbook*: "This is my recipe. Maybe it will work for you, maybe it won't. All good recipes have areas for each chef to add their own spices, their own flavor, their own pizzazz! You need to find what will work for you." From the "Skateboard Sub Sandwich," to the "Comfort Zone Zucchini Cupcakes," Earnshaw's *The EduCulture Cookbook* is brimming with recipes you can use TODAY. Get your hands on a copy and start working with your school team to whip up the most delicious, attractive recipes for school culture you can imagine. I promise you that everyone will be begging for seconds!

— DR. JEFF PRICKETT - HIGH SCHOOL PRINCIPAL

This is a book all educators should read. It's full of applicable ideas that anyone could implement and help them to improve. In addition, each section of the book has personal stories that Mike describes that are relatable to anyone in the education field. Any educator that is looking for some fresh ideas will enjoy this book. It's fun, easy to read, and clever!

— Dr. Nick Sutton - Superintendent and Author

Although you may not be a chef in the kitchen, you are going to be a master of educational recipes after reading *The EduCulture Cookbook*. Michael Earnshaw is a fantastic storyteller as he shares his leadership and classroom experiences to provide practical, pertinent, and relevant strategies. The EduCulture Cookbook provides an incredible guide for educators on cultural investments, personnel connections, and valuing others. You will not want to miss out on this wonderful resource to positively increase your school and classroom culture!

— Joshua Stamper, Assistant Principal, Speaker, Teach Better Podcast Network Manager, and host of the Aspire Podcast

Copyright © 2021 by Michael Earnshaw
Published by EduMatch®
PO Box 150324, Alexandria, VA 22315
www.edumatchpublishing.com

All rights reserved. No portion of this book may be reproduced in any form without permission from the publisher, except as permitted by U.S. copyright law. For permissions contact sarah@edumatch.org.

These books are available at special discounts when purchased in quantities of 10 or more for use as premiums, promotions fundraising, and educational use. For inquiries and details, contact the publisher: sarah@edumatch.org.

ISBN: 978-1-953852-37-3

THE EDUCULTURE COOKBOOK

RECIPES & DISHES TO POSITIVELY TRANSFORM
SCHOOL & CLASSROOM CULTURE

MICHAEL EARNSHAW

Foreword by
JEFF KUBIAK

CONTENTS

Foreword — xv
Jeff Kubiak — Author of One Drop of Kindness, and It's Me | Equity and Inclusion Champion and Educator.

Introduction — xvii

1. Skateboard Sub Sandwich — 1
2. Prison Break Pie — 13
3. Popsicles for Breakfast — 25
4. Spicy Speed Dating Soup — 37
5. Struggle Island Stew — 49
6. Literature-O-Lanterns Lasagna — 57
7. Weakness Waffles — 67
8. Hansel & Gretel's Crumb Cake — 75
9. Texting Toast — 85
10. Comfort Zone Zucchini Cupcakes — 93
11. Selfless Sliders — 107
12. Flippin' Flapjacks — 117
13. Pop Punk Passion Pizza — 131
14. Red Velvet Video Vlogs — 143
15. Summer Selfie Sangria — 153

Acknowledgments — 161
About the Author — 163
References — 165

This book is dedicated to all of the educators that are making connections, sharing their passions, and putting relationships first to make a difference in the lives of our students every single day. Our students need you more than you know. Keep inspiring, empowering, and changing their lives for the positive. Never give up.

To all of the staff that I have been blessed to work with, thank you for going along with my crazy antics and punk rock approach to changing students' lives. You are my inspiration to keep going every day.

To my beautiful wife, Megan, I thank you with all of my heart for always sticking by me and being my voice of reason. You truly should receive a paycheck of your own as a consultant from our district if they only knew how much advice you've provided me. I can't imagine this ride without you. I love you more than you'll ever know.

To my two amazing kids, Evan and Aubrey. You both teach me so much every single day, more than I ever let you know. I hope that you always find happiness in everything you do. Always put people first, help them with your strengths, rely on them where you have areas to grow, never give up, and always be true to yourself. I know you both will change this world and I will always be your biggest cheerleader!

FOREWORD

JEFF KUBIAK — AUTHOR OF ONE DROP OF KINDNESS, AND IT'S ME | EQUITY AND INCLUSION CHAMPION AND EDUCATOR.

I first connected with the EduChef, Mike Earnshaw, in the Spring of 2019 via Twitter. I'm not sure which group we were both in, but perhaps it was #PrincipalsInAction, or #TeachBetter, or #LeadLap. Whichever one, we both had plenty in common. We had been teachers, and at the time, were both Elementary School Principals with very similar values, missions, and passions for leading others. I knew instantly that there was something special about Mr. Earnshaw. Mike's passion for empowering teachers and students was different. It wasn't canned, bottled, faked, or improvised. It was and is, true and honest. His love of education, learning, and leading seems to be in his DNA. While I've never been at one of his schools, Mike's leadership style is well known in the education circles. He has a true charisma and is willing to risk a lot of himself in a truly selfless manner to help others -- all others, not his favorites, but every child, and adult that comes into his building.

Mike and I finally met in person in November 2019 at the 1st Annual Teach Better Conference in Cuyahoga Falls, OH. We were both there to present sessions, but also to hang out, get to know each other, and learn from each other's failures and triumphs. It was after just a few days of spending time with the EduChef that I knew. This dude was epic!

There are a LOT of educational leadership books to choose from these days, but *The EduCulture Cookbook* is different. Not only does it have stories of why Mike does what he does, or how he shares his passion and perspectives, but it also gives the reader an insight into what makes an entire school culture better. You'll read vignettes from impassioned teachers and recipes and ingredients of what makes an engaging staff meeting. You may laugh, and go "aha," or you may even shed a tear during "Struggle Island," but know this: This is an educational self- and community-help guide. Some of the stories, and recipes seem so simple, and "no brainer," perhaps. But, you will quickly learn of the relevance, connectedness, reality, passion, and authenticity that make this a guide and journey, not "just another PD book."

So hold on my friends. What you are about to embark upon is a cookbook full of love, passion, and power to a better way of education and life. The smiles, skateboarding, wipeouts, rail grabs, and educational fireworks will make you pining for more. Thank you for joining me on this journey, and be ready to be inspired like never before!

INTRODUCTION

We've all been asked the question, "If you didn't go into education, what would you have done?" For me, that's a simple answer, culinary school. I would have, and was very close to, enrolling in culinary school and becoming a chef.

My passion for cooking and the Culinary Arts began in seventh grade. I entered Home Ec., excited that we would finally be cooking something over the stove. Today's delicacy: grilled cheese. Now, I had been cooking grilled cheese at home for about a year already. My mom taught me how, and aren't moms always the first teacher? Put the pan on the stovetop, medium heat. Drop a square of butter in the pan, circle it around as it melts, coating the entire area. Drop a piece of bread in the melted butter, spin it around three times. Place 1.5 slices of American Cheese on top, then top it off with another piece of bread. After the first side is grilled, remove the sandwich, drop in another square of butter, and drop in the uncooked side of the sandwich. Three spins and let it cook.

This day in Home Ec. I thought I would be King! I would get to showcase my grilled cheese skills to all of my peers! Today though, I was humbled. I learned that as good as Mom's recipe was, there were so many other variations and approaches to the simple sandwich, just as good, if not better! (Don't worry, my mom got a copy of this book with no Introduction). I learned that to slow the burning of the butter some of my classmates spread it on the bread before tossing it in the pan. Some students used two pieces of cheese. Some, get this craziness, used two DIFFERENT types of cheese like cheddar and mozzarella! I was in awe, and couldn't wait to get home and cook up all of these different versions and create some new ones of my own.

I continued to cook simple meals at home, and once high school hit I got my first job as a busboy. This led me to become a dishwasher in the kitchen, then a Prepper, to Assistant Cook, and finally Head Line Cook. I held this position for about 15 years! I led the kitchen during college and student teaching, even though our advisors discouraged it. I didn't quit because (1) I needed money and (2) I loved it! I loved the connections and unity I had with my co-workers and I loved hearing how much the customers enjoyed the dish I had prepared, cooked, and then served for them. I learned so many recipes from the various owners and managers I worked under, and also had the go-ahead to put a little of my flavor into the recipes! The happier the customer was with their dish, the better the tip for our waitresses, and the better the chance they would not only tell their friends to visit us and get a bite to eat, but they would also be back themselves.

Education isn't any different. We want our customers to keep coming back. If you're a teacher, it's students, and if administrator, it's staff that are our returning customers. We want them to finish everything on their plates, and share stories with their friends and families of how delicious the meals we prepared for them were. We want them to keep thinking back, remembering the impression that meal had on them. How do we do this as educators? Through our lessons and activities.

The educational culture-transforming recipes I'm about to share with you have all been cooked up in my "kitchen" and have all had rave reviews from my "customers." Sure, I've cooked up some doozies; we all do now and then. Those aren't included in these pages. I'm sure I'll go back and give them another go; they may work out next time, maybe not. But the recipes in the following pages, these have been culture changers for us. These have helped to successfully transform us in such a short amount of time into a group of educators that rely on each other, collaborate, support, and encourage one another to be the best for kids. All kids. Every kid. Sure, I've served these dishes as an Elementary School Principal to my staff. But the beauty in these dishes is they can be devoured by anyone! Every time I cook up a dish, my goal is that not only our staff learns from and enjoys it, but they can also in turn take the recipe back to their classrooms and students with a little flavor of their own.

After each story, you'll find a recipe card with a QR code. These recipe cards are for those times, a few months later after you've finished the book, when you want to revisit an idea but can't find it through all of your highlights and Post-It notes. Save them to your phone, print them out, but use them as a reference when you want to cook something up for your staff or students.

Please don't feel you need to follow these recipes to a T. Like my grilled cheese experience, there are many different approaches, spices, and ingredients for each recipe. With that being said, I need to thank all of the educators that have influenced and helped shape the recipes to fit our school. Some have been created by scratch by me while others are old-time game changers that I added some of my spices to.

As you read our stories, think of ways to serve them to your customers. Tweet out those spices that stick out to you, or those you add on your own. Share pictures and stories of how well they go over. If you get stuck, reach out to me. I'm always here to help spice up a dish.

Mike Earnshaw
@MikeREarnshaw
#EduCultureCookbook

1

SKATEBOARD SUB SANDWICH

I'm not the first principal to bring a skateboard into school and shred down the hallways and I definitely won't be the last. I've gotten some flack from others saying I'm just trying to copy Hamish Brewer, the Tattooed Skateboarding Principal. Now I can't lie. Hamish is a huge influence and factor in me sharing my love of skateboarding with our students, staff, and families. I've credited him many times when this comes up when I'm questioned about skateboarding on podcasts or speaking gigs. If it weren't for seeing Hamish stay true to himself while empowering a school, I might have left my deck in my garage. I have skateboarded since I was eight years old, and it was time I embraced my love and grind it into my "work." My original reasoning for bringing my love of skateboarding into our school was to simply bring some fun to our halls and classrooms. It has accomplished this, but there are so many more benefits that I wasn't even expecting!

As I sat on top of the wooden planked house at our local park, enthralled at what I saw in the distance, the refreshing spring breeze tossed my bleached blonde mopped hair, my jaw resting in my lap. Kids were launching themselves off of the swings, older siblings pushing their younger ones at breakneck speeds on the merry-go-round, and numerous games of tag were in play while the moms socialized on the stationary benches surrounding the playing field.

"Michael...Michael...what are you doing? Why aren't you playing?"

It was my mom yelling. I don't know how many times she called my name, or for how long, but it wasn't of importance to me. I had to have been around five years old. I didn't have any sisters at the time yet and was an only child.

"Michael, what is wrong? Do you need help getting down?" she pleaded from down below.

I didn't understand how anyone else wasn't amazed by what was happening in the prairie across the street. How was I the only one completely mesmerized by four teenagers skateboarding on a six-foot halfpipe? At the time, I didn't know it was six feet. It wasn't until a few years later when I got to skate this beast of a ramp myself!

Without even glancing down at my mom, I murmured, "Mom, I'm watching them skateboard!"

That day at the park was a turning point in my life. From then on, I wanted nothing more than to become a skateboarder. I begged and pleaded with my parents, continually being told I was too young and that it was too dangerous, and "You'll break a bone!" This was my version of Ralphie in "A Christmas Story," how he does everything in his power to convince his parents, teacher, and a mall Santa that he needs a Red Ryder BB Gun for Christmas. Everyone kept telling Ralphie, "You'll shoot your eye out kid!"

A few months went by and we were visiting my grandma's house for a backyard summer bbq. My dad's youngest brother was in his early twenties. I don't know if the other cousins felt how I did, but I thought he was just the coolest. Young, going to concerts every weekend, into comic books and horror movies, and on this blistering July afternoon, he gave me a gift that forever changed my life.

"Hey Mike, go into the garage and check out what's next to the door, the one that goes to the backyard," my uncle said.

I gave him a somewhat confused look because he never gave me a gift unless it was my birthday or Christmas. Today was neither.

I walked into the garage, which was about fourteen degrees warmer than that out on the sidewalk, and saw, leaning up against the wall a black plastic skateboard with yellow wheels! It wasn't new. I could see the black dirt marks from previous rides on the wheels, but it was so cool!

I grabbed the board with both hands and ran to my uncle. "Bobby, can I ride it?"

He chuckled and said, "Yeah, of course. You can have it, I don't need it anymore."

I can't tell you how many miles I put in on that skateboard. It was a small penny board, probably from the '70s, and I couldn't do any tricks on it, just cruise around my neighborhood, feeling free. My parents grew warm to the fact that I was going to be a skateboarder after seeing my determination and grit to not give up.

A few years went by, I had gone through a few more cheap plastic skateboards from Toys-R-Us and KMart, never really getting a quality one to do tricks on. For me, I was enjoying just skating and cruising, ripping through the air, floating down the street, but the urge to do what I witnessed those teenagers do in that prairie years back never escaped my mind.

"Mom, for Christmas, all I want, seriously, I don't want anything else, is a professional skateboard!"

"Alright, we'll see, they're expensive," was mom's response.

In desperation, I stated, "I don't care, that's all I want, seriously, please?"

Christmas morning came and like every child, I was up about 1.5 hours before my parents said I could be. Honestly, I snuck downstairs a few times to see if there was a skateboard. I saw some gifts with my name on it, but none that even resembled the shape of a skateboard.

The rest of the family finally got up, but at this point, my zest for opening gifts was gone. I had already opened all of the small gifts in my head. I still went through the motions to appease my parents and younger sisters, but inside I was crying, devastated. The one thing I wanted wasn't here.

"Hey Mike, hold on, I think there's something in the garage," my dad said as he returned from the kitchen with a fresh cup of Maxwell House.

I didn't hesitate. I darted to the garage, replaying that scene in "A Christmas Story" where Ralphie finds that Red Ryder BB Gun he so desperately longed for. There it was! In the middle of the floor was a brand new, Ray Underhill, Powell Peralta skateboard! My jaw dropped lower than it had that day I first was in awe of the sport at the park. I'm surprised that the speed of my jaw's drop-in didn't shatter the cold-concrete garage floor.

I was never the best skater, but that didn't matter to me. I enjoyed learning new tricks, spending every Friday and Saturday night with my friends in empty parking lots, grinding and railing over waxed up parking blocks under the dim street lights. We would stay in a spot as long as we could. Once the police rolled up, we were always polite and went on our way. This was long before every town had a FREE outdoor skatepark. In my heyday, skateparks were only for those days when it was raining or winter weather months where snow and sub-zero temps engulfed the Earth.

Skateboarding stayed a part of my life into my college years, where I transitioned into more of solely a vert skater. If you're wondering what vert skating is, think of Tony Hawk. He has made his entire skateboarding career skating vert, large halfpipe ramps that resemble a "U." Now I have never taken on the monster vert ramps that Tony has. The largest I've ever skated was six feet and that was a beautifully scary rush! My hat is off to the amazing feats Tony Hawk and many others can accomplish. Once my children were brought into this world, skateboarding began taking somewhat of a backseat, but I always found time to do a few flatland tricks in front of our house.

For me, skateboarding is not only an outlet, an escape from what is clouding my head. It is a way to express myself, to challenge and push myself, and to build bonds with others that are thicker than blood.

Why had I been hiding this part of my life, which helped to mold me into the leader, father, husband, and individual that I am? Once I finally brought skateboarding into my role as an educational leader, EVERYONE benefited. Our staff, families, and most importantly our STUDENTS saw a piece of me, as an individual. They saw a principal, cruising around the halls and campus, teaching students about skateboarding and tricks, not afraid to share who he was. This helped to break down so many walls for everyone, walls that were hiding others from being true to who they were and embracing and enjoying their opportunity to make a difference every day.

At first, I had my skateboard with me and Adina (you'll learn more about her in another recipe). My board and I would make our rounds around the school. Sometimes if I needed to get to another side of the school quickly, I'd grab my board, leave Adina behind, and skate there. The kids got a kick out of it, seeing me roll through the halls in a shirt and tie. It was something fun we all shared. Students were proud to tell their parents that their principal was a skater, riding a skateboard around in a shirt and tie, and how they wanted to get one too.

During recess or after school, I would do some basic flatland tricks on the playground: ollies, shove-its, crab walks, and manuals. Kids started asking me about skateboarding, how to do the tricks I do, how long I have been skateboarding for, could I teach them, and do I fall a lot.

The last question is one of my favorites. I've been able to turn it into a very teachable moment. Every time I'm asked if I fall, I give the same response.

"Of course, I fall all the time, especially when I'm learning a new trick. I even fall when trying to do tricks I've been able to do for

30 years. The thing is, I never give up. I never stop trying. I will fall and fail, and I always get back up and try again. That's what we need to do in life. No matter what, never give up."

By sharing a passion of mine with our students and staff, I was able to make connections and teach lessons about learning from failure, having a PMA (Positive Mental Attitude), and to keep working towards our goals. I also was able to build stronger relationships with students that wouldn't let anyone else into their lives.

We had a student in our school that struggled for many years, academically, but more so behaviorally. The teachers the student had were phenomenal, always trying to make that breakthrough into what was the driving force behind the student's misbehavior and choices. Once one made a little headway, it always was shut down by this student.

"Hey Mr. E, I have a skateboard, can I bring mine to school?" I heard faintly from outside a classroom door not far from where Adina and I were working.

"Come on over here," I replied, shutting my laptop to show I was fully engaged in our conversation.

"You skateboard? I'll tell you what, you can bring it on Friday...."

I was quickly cut off with a smile and excitement. "Really? Awesome!"

I continued, "You didn't let me finish. You can bring it IF you earn it. I'm going to work with your teacher and create a chart where if you earn five stamps for the week, you can bring your skateboard. There are a few rules if you earn it. You have to let me keep it in my office, no riding in the halls. Then, at the end of the day, we can go out on the blacktop and I'll teach you a few tricks."

Our friend earned his five stamps that week. And the next. And the next after that even after upping the requirement to eight stamps, then ten. Every time we went out on the blacktop, we skated around together, discussed tricks, attempted some, and then talked. We talked about our lives, failures, successes, the future, fears, and happiness. We built a relationship where we trusted each other and truly wanted to see each other succeed. This was extremely beneficial when our friend didn't make the best choices. He knew that the consequences I put forth for his actions were for his best interest. He knew they weren't truly consequences, but opportunities to learn from and grow. He knew I wanted to help guide him to change his poor choices, to know how to make better ones in the future, and see him become more than anyone else has ever thought for him.

"I think the skateboard helps you focus. There must be something about always being in motion." This was told to me by a staff member I have known since I entered the district as an Assistant Principal at our Junior High. This statement has been told to me over and over by others, even from some of my crew that I've never met face to face. And it's true. Ever since I was a young kid on that penny board from my uncle, just cruising around on a skateboard, the feeling of slicing through the air, not being able to be stopped on a smooth ride, has always brought me zen.

I am not recommending all of you bring a skateboard into your classrooms and schools and start skating around. This is my recipe. Maybe it will work for you, maybe it won't. All good recipes have areas for each chef to add their own spices, their own flavor, their own pizzazz! You need to find what will work for you. What passion of yours can you bring in to share with colleagues, families, and students. What passion will help you to build strong connections, provide learning opportunities, and bring a smile to not only their faces but yours?

That's what this cookbook is about. These are the recipes that have helped me fully love my role as an educator. These recipes have worked for me to transform our school and classroom cultures for the positive. I'm going to be providing you the basic ingredients, and it's up to you to throw your own spices into each dish!

SKATEBOARD SUB SANDWICH

INGREDIENTS

1. Passionate hobby
2. Skateboard (or any ingredient related to YOUR passionate hobby)
3. Travel bag
4. Desire to share a passionate hobby with others
5. Openness discussing passionate hobby with others

PREP TIME

- Prep Time - 1 minute
- Cook Time - 6 - 7 hours
- Total Time - 6 - 7 hours 1 minute
- Total Cost $120

PROCEDURE

1. Have a passionate hobby, an activity, that you use for your self-care. Something that releases all the stresses of life.
2. Gather any materials that relate to your passionate activity & place in a travel bag.
3. Bring passionate hobby materials to school with you.
4. Share your passionate hobby with your students &/or staff.
5. Share your passionate hobby as much as you want. I prefer daily if it fits.
6. Answer any questions students &/or staff may have about your passionate hobby.
7. Converse with others about your passionate hobby.
8. Discover ways to partake in & share completing your passionate hobby with others.

Cruising the Halls
By Christina Gaura
@RTI158
Reading Specialist

When I first heard that Mike was now riding around the school on a skateboard, I was not surprised. Mike's a cool principal! He had already openly shared stories with staff about his youth and green hair days. He had committed himself to being visible and present for kids by using a rolling portable desk and laptop computer. Often, he was found, sitting in the back of classrooms, working on his computer. While working, he was immersing himself in the classroom setting and informally participating in student learning. I had witnessed the kids' excitement in daily seeing him in the hallway or their classrooms. He always had a fist bump, smile, high five, or kind word for every student.

I wondered about safety with the skateboard. However, the first time I stepped out of my classroom to watch him go down the hall on his board, in perfect control, I saw this was not a problem. Skateboarding was a beautiful example of a personal passion that Mike could share with the student body. He rode up on his board, and we talked about it. Mike truly wanted to know what I thought about his boarding. He radiated calm. I told him it was so apparent that after riding the board that he was somehow more himself. I told him I could see how happy the skateboard made him and how in control, grounded, and overall calmed he seemed.

I have since seen Mike many times engaging students through his skateboard, especially sharing this passion with some of our students that need a role model. Mike is dedicated to creating a welcoming and engaging learning environment where all are encouraged to be their best selves. If you are looking for Mike, he can be found skateboarding down the hallways of Oak Glen School, dragging his wheeled desk, on his way to save the day!

2

PRISON BREAK PIE

Let me preface this recipe that I have never been given a prison sentence within our correctional system. I do not have any first-hand knowledge of what goes on inside a prison within the United States other than what I have read in books, both fiction and non, or have seen on television. This recipe is not meant to bring any disrespect or mocking towards anyone that has gone through a prison sentence or has known a loved one that has. Instead, we can all become prisoners of our own mind, and that is what *Prison Break Pie* is about.

Prison sentences are never that bad at first. Like any new situation we're thrown into, whether it's of our own accord or not, there's that awkwardness that permeates throughout our air. The glares from every set of eyes as you enter your new "home" for whatever length of time you've been sentenced, heckles from others who have already taken up residence, believing that you don't have what it takes to make it in the "joint,"

taunts and threats shouted and echoed as you slumber through the bland, cold, gray halls for the first time to remind you that no matter what status you believe you hold, you're at the bottom of the food chain. Others have been residents long before you, and many will remain after you make it out, if you make it out.

Many school administrators would fare well, and actually enjoy time in the "clink." It is a very structured facility, where your daily routines run like clockwork. Every morning your cell door, as well as every other in the prison, unlock and open at the same time in unison. You step out, greet everyone within your vicinity with a smile and nod, and then head to breakfast. Here, you get your coffee, spend some time socializing with the same individuals you do every morning. Each day the conversation is different, but it's the same. You're just biding time until you're back in your small four walls.

After your coffee break, you make it back to your cell. The door is open, but you don't have the freedom to just leave, or at least that's what you believe. You spend the next few hours reading, writing, and doing what you have convinced yourself that you are supposed to be doing during these morning hours. You're spending time with yourself "catching up" on what you think needs to get done.

Before lunch hits is when you get to make your rounds. A brief stroll to get another cup of watered-down Joe, a step outside in the courtyard to get a little bit of sunshine. Maybe a quick workout or pickup game of basketball. Within the blink of an eye, you're back in your cell, acting as if the reading and writing have built up to catastrophic proportions while you were out.

You get in another hour or so, thinking you've made some headway, and then return to the Mess Hall. Meal times are the only moments that flash by. You're supposed to have a quality 45 minutes to yourself, but by the time your food has been engulfed it's back to the daily, dreadful grind. Again, time begins to stand still.

After lunch there's more downtime reading and writing. It never seems to end. No matter how many hours you dedicate to these time-consuming tasks, there's always more. In all honesty, it's been self-created. This is what you feel you need to do with your new role. It's what we've seen portrayed in television shows and movies. We put the stereotypical expectations we think others want to see us doing. You'll share some of your pieces with others, but many times they don't want to take the time, or they feel as if they are drowning in work themselves. You'll get a reply from some, others you need to hunt down and ask a few times face-to-face. At the end of the day, you can put away your journal and books and relax a little.

During the later hours of the day, you have some dinner with friends, watch some mind-numbing shows on television, and wind down for the night. Before "Light's Out," you may read a little bit for pleasure, dreaming of better days. Then you'll close your eyes just to wake up and do it all over again tomorrow. Like clockwork.

I lost three years doing this after I was sentenced. This wasn't how it was supposed to end for me. Each day that passed I began to get inside of my own head. That was the worst part, knowing that this would be my life for the next 20 or so years…unless I broke out. I told myself that was my only option for clarity, for sanity.

The funny thing about prisons is not that you are locked inside with a strict structure and routine. That's fine. The true prison is your own mind, your own thoughts. That's where the agony and anguish lies. Thinking how tomorrow, and the tomorrow after that, will be the same as today. **Our minds are the prisons that we cannot escape. It's up to us and us alone to free ourselves from whatever is holding us back and locking us in.** I needed to break out; it was the only solution if I was going to make it where my actions had brought me.

The prison I described above was one that I had chosen for myself. It was my goal to become a building principal. Since I had begun coursework for my Master's in Educational Administration, I fell in love with leading and inspiring staff. When I began the program I never had any intention of leaving the classroom, I was only doing it for the credentials and to get a bump on the teaching salary schedule. Quickly I realized the much larger impact I could have in education and touch many more lives of students by leading a building.

After my coursework was completed, I was fortunate to earn the title of Assistant Principal for a two-year run. This wasn't much different than my time as a classroom teacher. I was in classrooms daily, building relationships with staff and students. I was able to work hand-in-hand with others and positively change the lives of over 300 students, which was much more than the 90 I had as a middle-school ELA teacher.

The principalship is a different monster. Nothing could have prepared me for all of the behind the scenes paperwork and minutiae that accompanies the leader of a school. At first, I did my best to get out and build relationships. Since I was a child, I have always known the key to changing the world is meaningful, trusting, and sincere relationships. But as my first year as an elementary building principal began to unfold into the later months, I was finding myself spending more time in my prison cell.

The paperwork was overwhelming. There always seemed to be something else that needed to be completed and submitted to my supervisors. I also saw the number of emails that my fellow principals were sending to their staff daily. They were all much more seasoned than I was, and I believed that to be effective, so I needed to follow their suit.

I felt like I was Bill Murray in Groundhog Day. Three years had passed, three years I would never get back. Three years that I don't feel I was the best leader for my staff, or more importantly, our students. I was miserable. I was depressed. I began contemplating my choices and if there was any other career field I could enter with the credentials and skill sets I had. This was not why I had entered education. This was not why I had worked so hard to become a building principal. I told myself that I could not spend any more years trapped inside my cell, making phone calls, replying to emails, and creating and submitting meaningless documents. I declared I had two choices:

1. End it all and leave the field of education.
2. Break out of my cell and lead how I had always believed in my heart.

Year three ended and I had taken a lot of vacation days during June and July to self-reflect, find myself, and plan my escape. My heart was telling me that I was destined to change the lives of many and that serving as a principal was what I needed to do. I wasn't done yet.

I realized that many of the paperwork tasks I thought I needed to complete daily were just enemies I created in my mind. I knew that for me to be free and live out my vision of changing the world, I needed to get back to forming relationships. I needed to get out of my front office and spend as much time as I could in the hallways and classrooms amongst our amazing staff and inspiring students. Many ideas were formulated in my brain, but there was only one that I knew would be the perfect solution for myself. Once she entered my mind, I knew there was no other path to take to break out of my prison. Adina would be my savior!

Close your eyes and imagine being the only one in your school. It's silent, no noise is polluting the clean air of the hallways. Then, with the snap of your fingers, you hear plastic wheels rolling over the tiles of the hallway. It's loud, the "thud, thud, thud" takes over and pushes out whatever peaceful thoughts were dancing in your mind.

"Uuummm...what is that? It's so loud!" was what everyone had asked the first time they met Adina.

A smile always grew across my face before I answered. "This is Adina, my mobile desk!"

"That's cool, but what about your office?" questioned many.

"The school is my office," was the only explanation they needed.

I know I may sound like a broken Rancid record, but to me, relationships are everything. **To truly make a difference in the lives of others, and the bigger picture of changing the world, we must have relationships.** I've spent my entire career, sans the first three years as a principal, putting relationships first. It served me well and many lives were transformed. It's time to do that again.

After many plans and ideas, it hit me that the best way to get back into the hallways and classrooms, and still get all of my work done, was to get a mobile desk. She's nothing fancy, a section to place my laptop, a little cabinet for pens and pencils, #KINDNESS bands to pass out to students, and jeans passes for staff. There's also a section to place my skateboard and display what books I'm currently reading for all to see.

The first few weeks that Adina was with me was a learning curve for some. Classes would exit their room for a bathroom break or a Special's class and there we were, working at an intersection of hallways. When I needed to satisfy that hunger of the excitement that fills a classroom, we could easily roll into any of our choosing and spend time working and being visible and part of the learning.

"I need to talk to you…uuummm…are you in your office?" asked a teacher as I was in the middle of the hallway.

"Yeah, this is my office. What's up?" was my response.

She then took a step forward, breaking through the invisible threshold to engage in a conversation.

As time went on, staff and students understood my new concept and became comfortable talking and working together with me anywhere in the school. Of course, if there was a confidential conversation that needed to be had, we would step inside a closed-door room, but these were few and far between.

Besides connecting with others and building relationships, I noticed many positive changes that came with the addition of Adina, many that I hadn't even imagined when we began our dance together.

1. My inbox had significantly fewer emails. No longer were notifications and messages of small fires that were requesting my extinguishing. Being available and visible, I was able to take care of these flames well before they erupted into a full-blown blaze.
2. Student behavior improved. With being nearby at all times, I could hear if there was a disruption brewing inside of a classroom. A student walking out of a classroom in anger or frustration, no problem. I was right there.
3. I knew what was happening in our classrooms. I knew the lessons and content being taught, and I was invited to be a participant in these lessons much more frequently. If something amazing was taking place and I wasn't invited, I just crashed it!

It's been nearly two years and Adina and I are still together. Students love her and have given us personalized decorations to dress her in. If it wasn't for her, I'd either be miserable, locked inside of my prison of an office, or have left education completely. Had that happened, I would still be miserable and just contained inside a cubicle.

You don't have to serve a life sentence stuck inside of your office. Find someone, or something, that will break you out and show you the beauty of the landscape freedom that lies before you. For me, that was Adina, and I am forever grateful.

PRISON BREAK PIE

INGREDIENTS

1. A desire to be amongst students & staff
2. At least $120
3. Internet Access
4. Credit/Debit Card
5. Portable Desk

PREP TIME

- Prep Time - 30-45 minutes
- Cook Time - 6 hours
- Total Time - 180 school days
- Total Cost $110.00

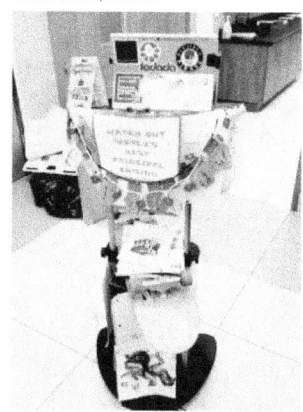

PROCEDURE

1. Accept the fact that we aren't supposed to sit behind a desk & computer every day, especially when we're supposed to be changing student lives.
2. Go to your favorite office supply shopping website.
3. Search "Mobile Desk."
4. Find a mobile desk style that fits your personality & needs.
5. Purchase desk with a credit/debit card.
6. Wait eagerly for delivery!
7. Assemble the mobile desk yourself (much more satisfying).
8. Equip mobile desk with necessary office equipment, e.g., stapler, pens, paper, paperclips, etc.
9. Leave your usual desk space daily, moving to new locations with the mobile desk.

Unexpected Benefits to Being Out of Your Office
By Mark French
@PrincipalFrench
Principal

When I connected with the #PrincipalsInAction group, I enjoyed the challenges of getting out of the office and being a more visible, fun, and present leader. I used to think being a good administrator meant staying in my office waiting to respond to phone calls, email messages, and drop-in visitors to answer questions and solve problems. But, getting out of my office resulted in some unexpected benefits.

First, I expected that being out of my office in hallways, in classrooms, on the playground, in the cafeteria, and at arrival and dismissal would enhance my visibility and strengthen relationships, but I discovered unexpected benefits. Getting to know students and watch how they are doing socially and academically proved invaluable. During conferences, IEP meetings, and student assistance team meetings, I was able to share direct experiences with students. I think it's powerful when the principal can talk about a student's strengths and needs with teachers and family members based on their personal interactions and relationship.

How can a leader influence and create practices and procedures if they aren't out of their office observing and learning? I loved being on the playground, in the cafeteria, in the hallways, and at arrival and dismissal observing traffic flow, student movement, schedules, the clock, and boy, was that helpful. I was able to observe playground supervisors needing more direction and professional development and we provided that. I was able to observe ineffective and effective drop-off and pick-up patterns and addressed those. I watched cafeteria lines and service and was able to influence positive changes. Being out of your office allows a leader to observe, learn, and make changes.

Another benefit of being out of your office is to pay attention to the physical spaces and needs of your building and grounds. Don't just be on the playground, but walk the perimeter and visit all areas of your school grounds. By doing this, I was able to influence and improve landscaping, get cracked sidewalks and parking lots repaired, advocate for a new school sign, identify places for outdoor learning, and secure funds for a greenhouse addition to the school building. Inside, I saw the floor and wall tiles that needed repairing, stained ceiling panels that needed replacing, and doors and windows that needed cleaning. You can't notice these things sitting in your office.

One last benefit of being a leader who makes it a priority to be out of the office is having the ability to observe teaching and learning in order to support your staff. I've made curricular, materials, resource, staffing, and professional development decisions to support teachers and students based on observing in classrooms and talking to teachers and students.

You will definitely increase your visibility and relationships by making it a priority to be out of your office and hopefully you will experience other unexpected benefits as I have.

3

POPSICLES FOR BREAKFAST

Adina and I spent a glorious 180 days together. As a team, we helped to transform the culture of our building. We were able to make a statement, make our names known, our presence felt. All of the staff, and more importantly, the students, knew that we were the dynamic duo and we're there to help make their days better. We helped to solve problems where others struggled, mend broken relationships, and return smiles to frowned faces. Like the hibernation habits of bears, Adina falls into a deep slumber during the summer months when the halls are eerily silent and being dressed in fresh coats of wax.

The start of a school year is always an exciting time for educators, families, and students. Fresh starts. New relationships. Mile-high goals. Excitement for learning. Smiles galore. Adina was ready to break out of her den, and I was just as ecstatic to start cruising the halls with her. We were ready for new artwork and lasting memories to be made these next 180 days. I decided to have a conversation with my social worker who always has a way of putting everything into perspective when I only see the "rainbows and unicorns," as she says.

"How do you think you did last year, with visiting classrooms?" she asked in a tone as if she had already seen the answer through her crystal ball earlier that morning.

"What do you mean? Great! I was only in my front office like 2% of the school year last year," was my matter-of-fact-in-your-face-reply.

She let out a sigh like she knew she had to teach me the lesson that I already should know but won't admit it. "Mike, that's not what I asked. Yes, you were very visible, always in the halls, working with everyone. **But how were you with visiting classrooms? Was it even? Were some visited more than others? If you looked at your Twitter or Instagram feed would it be a pretty equal representation with pictures?**" She then gazed at me, knowing the answers had now been uncovered inside of me.

Wow, did I just dig myself into a hole that I was going to need to tunnel my way out of? There was no ladder made of twine and twigs that could reach me here. My only option was to begin clawing my way through the dirt, creating channels to find a new escape route to reach the sunlight.

"Uuummm...well...yeah...I got pictures of every classroom," was my not-so-confident-you-already-know-I'm-full-of-it reply.

I could sense the frustration through her voice and body language as she shifted in her seat. "Yeah, you got a lot of pictures, but was it mostly the same classes over and over? Were some pictured way more than others," she questioned with the answers right there in the words she quietly and passively shouted.

I knew that I was not going to win this battle. "Fine, yes, I guess I did keep visiting the same classrooms over and over. That's what I need to work on. I need to get into every class evenly. How can I do that?"

"That's up to you, but I think the great things you began last year are only going to get better and stronger if you commit to getting into every classroom and showcasing teachers equally. How you do it is up to you," and the conversation was over. I knew from her statement there was nothing more I could say. I now needed to leave her office and figure out how to ensure I did what needed to be done.

"Did you ever notice that you call on students from the right side of the classroom 95% of the time and the left only 5%," was a question posed to me by my assistant principal during our post-observation conference while I was still an ELA teacher.

I glanced away from her and then stared at the whiteboard in her office decorated with letters forming words in various dry erase marker colors that were thoughts and tasks solely for her. It appeared I was reading the board, but in all actuality, I was reflecting on what she had asked me. I've never been good at making eye contact when I don't have an answer I'm confident in. Did I really only pick from one side of the room? Then I realized I had turned my head over my right shoulder for this contemplation.

"Do I really?" was my response. What else could I say; it was true. I favored the right side of my classroom for whatever reason. It wasn't that I enjoyed hearing from those students any more than the others. Throughout my life, I always seemed to pick what was more so on the right-hand side for me.

"Yes, you do. Look at how many times you called on each student. I sketched a draft of your room and marked each time you called on kids," was her answer as she plopped the data in front of me as if I was in an interrogation.

At this point, I had been in the game of education for a few years, and I knew there was only one way to save some face. There was one phrase that administrators loved to hear when they pointed out areas of growth in your teaching practice. I brought our eyes back together and with confidence declared what I know she yearned to hear.

"I'm going to work on that."

I needed to find a way to equally call on all of my students. No matter what funky-new-age-hippy desk setup I chose (as my colleagues called it), I would always favor the students seated on the right. I knew that I couldn't just trust myself to make sure I called on everyone equally. Old habits die hard, and this habit had been with me for about four years of teaching at this point. I needed help, I needed assistance, I needed a tool to help me get to every student. I remembered a conversation I had with my first teacher, a teacher of many, many years, my mom.

"Mike, what are you doing? Are you eating those banana popsicles?" my mom inquired in an unacceptable scowl.

I glanced down in front of me. On top of a napkin were 2 popsicle sticks, the condensation still soaking in through the wood. I took the last bite of my third, sucked down the deliciousness of the artificial banana flavoring, and lined my third stick next to the others.

"Mom, yeah, it's breakfast," was my I'm-still-your-son-and-I-can-eat-whatever-I-want-like-I'm-still-in-college-for-breakfast-even-though-I'm-back-living-under-your-roof reply.

"Michael," she screeched to let me know how serious she was. "You can't eat popsicles for breakfast, that's ridiculous. How old are you?"

Twenty-five was what I shouted in my head. What came out of my mouth was, "Fine, you're right," because I knew she was. Moms usually are.

As I went to throw away my breakfast that would better serve a seven-year-old on a spicy summer Saturday, I thought about what happens to all of the popsicle sticks that get thrown out. I pondered this for about seven seconds before tossing them in the garbage and heading off to change the lives of my students for the day.

"Today we're going to analyze the characters in *The Outsiders*. We want to look at which characters were dynamic and which were static," I said to my seventh grade ELA students.

I continued, "Ponyboy, why not start with him?"

Hands fired towards the decrepit ceiling. I scanned the room. Hands were up on the right-hand side, as well as the left. Each side of the classroom was equally represented and today was the first day that I would be able to ensure I heard from all of my students, regardless of what side of the classroom they sat on.

"Put your hands down, you're not going to need to raise them anymore," I declared with confidence like a superhero determined to save a city, cape floating behind me and all.

Their hands went down and their mouths opened as well.

I gave the traditional five-second pause, then shared, "I have notecards with all of your names on them. From now on I'm going to just pick from the cards for someone to answer. But before we get going with our discussion on dynamic and static characters, I need you to put some information on the back of your card."

I passed out everyone's card. I flicked to a new page on the SmartBoard that listed three statements:

1. Favorite candy
2. Favorite movie
3. Favorite band/song

"I need everyone to quickly put their answers on the back of their card and then pass them back to me."

Before 90 seconds escaped, I had everyone's card back in my hands and we began our discussion of dynamic and static characters based on S.E. Hinton's *The Outsiders*.

After utilizing these index cards for calling on my students, I learned they served many more functions than just getting to hear from everyone. For example they also:

1. Gave me an insight into my students' lives with the information they provided on the back.
2. They helped to randomly pick groups and partners.
3. If I set them in order before students entered class, I could pick groups and partners that I wanted, but we could say groups were "randomly" picked and that the cards picked who they wanted. Students believed this. I told them, "It was what the Universe wanted."

My social worker friend was right. I needed to get into every class, get pictures of every teacher and their students and share the amazing things happening in their rooms. I needed to give positive feedback to all of my staff equally to help propel all of us to be better for our students. Adina and I couldn't leave anyone behind.

I was writing a new blog at the kitchen table as my kids were winding down for bed. My wife and kids were relaxing on the couch, watching Spongebob, when my ears were blessed with the beautiful voice of my sweets-addicted daughter.

In a sing-song voice from the living room she yelled, "Dad, can I have a popsicle?"

"She can have one, they're not that bad for you," my wife said, answering the question I was about to ask before I could ask it. She's good at that, probably because she's a mom.

As I watched my daughter take that last bite off her popsicle, brandishing only the wooden stick it was served on in her hand, my mind's lightbulb ignited!

"Good morning! Do we have any popsicle sticks? Or index cards?" I asked my office staff before even putting my bag and skateboard down in my front office.

"Uuummm...good morning," and then a chuckle followed from my administrative assistant. "I think we have some in the back room. How many do you need and what are they for?"

"How many staff do we have in total?" I asked, and then opened the door to my office to put down my belongings. She came back with more than enough of the bigger style cards. "Perfect, can you do me a favor and write every staff member's name on one?" I asked.

She replied, "Of course. But what are these for again?"

A smile grew across my bearded face. "I am going to use them to pick three each day, and those are the rooms I will be visiting and showcasing!"

She now grew her own smile, only no beard. "Wow, that's a great idea!"

Since that day I have come into school every morning, dropped off my belongings, put my lunch in the fridge, and picked three popsicle sticks. After the morning announcements, I'll grab Adina the Mobile Desk and head to that first classroom that was randomly picked.

After spending time in the room, talking with students and learning alongside them, I'd be sure to get some pictures to post on our various social media sites. After a classroom or staff member was visited, their card goes into a separate pile. This helps to ensure that I don't stop in and spend time with them until I get through all of the sticks. Some days I get through all three rooms early and end up picking one or two more, whereas on other days I only get through one. The rooms I picked that I didn't make it to go back in the fresh pile. Maybe they'll get chosen again tomorrow, maybe next week. It's not my choice; it's the sticks. It's what the Universe wanted.

In a surprised and pleased tone, my social worker stated, "I'm impressed. You have made it to everyone, left feedback, and gotten pictures!"

"I told you I would, and I'm so glad I did!" was my reply. "And you know what else?"

"Oh sweet Jesus, what?"

"I sent a picture to Facebook yesterday (our District Office regulates what gets put on the District Facebook page), and they replied, 'Mike, I'm impressed, you've sent a picture of every single classroom to us!'"

"You know what I replied? Of course I did, that's part of telling our story, that's my job."

This conversation happened only 39 days into the year. Next time, I want to accomplish this by day 20!

We must showcase the amazing things that are happening in our classrooms. There is so much negativity in the media regarding teachers, schools, and education. They only portray one side of a story, the negative nuggets they may come across and then throw them in the oven like reverse Shrinky Dinks to grow to extra large pieces. **Every classroom has something amazing taking place.** It's our duty, regardless of our role, to share these amazing acts.

By constantly sharing what happens in every classroom at our school, I was able to share our story with parents. They learned about who we are, what our mission as a school is, and the passions of our staff. Parents and stakeholders get a better feeling of unity, like they are part of changing students' lives by seeing what we do. Now, when it nears the beginning of the school year, I no longer get any phone calls asking for students to be transferred to another teacher's class. Our families know that EVERY classroom is amazing, magical, engaging, safe, and fun.

Share your stories. Administrators don't just visit the classrooms of "those" teachers that are going above and beyond. Teachers, share what you're doing with your administrators. Invite them in, get pictures yourself, and send them to parents via Class Dojo, Remind, or any communication means you are comfortable with. **If we don't tell our world-changing stories someone else will, and I promise it will not be as good of a version as ours.**

POPSICLES FOR BREAKFAST

INGREDIENTS

1. Index Cards / Popsicle SticksBlack
2. Sharpie Marker
3. Cell Phone w/ camera & internet access

PREP TIME

- Prep Time - 33 minutes
- Cook Time - 10 minutes minimum
- Total Time - 50 minutes
- Total Cost - $2.99

PROCEDURE

1. Write down all of your staffs'/students' names on an index card/popsicle stick.
2. Put all index cards/popsicle sticks in a pile.
3. Each morning or each class period randomly pick index cards/popsicle sticks. Those will be the staff/students you visit/call upon.
4. When amazing learning opportunities arise, take a picture.
5. Post the amazing picture to various social media sites to share your story w/ stakeholders.
6. After the staff/student has been observed or called upon, place that index card/stick into a separate pile.
7. Once all index cards/popsicle sticks from the original pile have been gone through, start over again!

Bringing the Sense
By Melanie Toppmeyer, MSW, LCSW
School Social Worker

When I met Mike, I was fresh out of graduate school, ready to start my career as a first-year school social worker. I was hired as the social worker for Oak Glen Elementary in Lansing School District 158. Mike was transitioning roles from assistant principal at the junior high to principal at Oak Glen. So, although he often forgets the exact number of years he's worked at Oak Glen, I am there to remind him we started at the same time. Being the social worker, I work very closely with our administrative team. I learned quickly of Mike's "open-door policy," though this policy shifted slightly through the years, from him being in his office with the door open, to him walking the hallways and popping his head into classrooms, to him skateboarding in the hallways and giving fist bumps to the students. Regardless of how he made his connections, he has always had the motto of: "If you need something or you have an idea, feel free to approach and come talk to me. We will discuss your ideas together." As I became more assertive throughout my years at Oak Glen, I took him up on his open-door policy many times, asking questions, sharing ideas, or, to his delight I'm sure, giving my blunt and honest opinion on matters. This is how the popsicle stick idea came about.

Mike is proud of his staff at Oak Glen and loves to take pictures of the work we are doing with our students. Sometimes, these photos end up on the district social media pages or the district website. We have all kinds of talented people at Oak Glen —staff who are out of the box thinkers, staff who have impeccable organizational skills, staff with great structure and behavior management tactics, etc. I think this is what makes the education profession so special. Teachers do not all teach the same, and students do not all learn the same. At Oak Glen, we are lucky to have so many different personalities and teaching styles. I think it is important that all our staff get recognized for the work they do. So, when I voiced to Mike one day that he needed to make sure to get into all classrooms to observe and showcase the variety of teaching styles we have at Oak Glen, he ran with the idea and created the "popsicle system."

I am thankful for a principal who is willing to listen and make changes so that our school, our students, and our staff can continue to become the best version possible. Though he is the leader of the school, he often tells staff that we as a team make the biggest impact when we work together. He encourages us to leave our egos at the door, ask for help, and accept suggestions from others. As the principal, he follows his own advice as well. After all, as educators, we are not meant to stay the same. We are meant to change, improve, and make an impact.

4

SPICY SPEED DATING SOUP

I am a faithful husband of 13 years. Before my beautiful, amazing wife and I tied the knot, we were together for 9 years. So basically, if you're doing the math, we have been together for 22 years! Sure, during those 9 we went on our own "Break"; I mean, that was the era of "Friends." Still, we always knew that we were each other's soul mates, peanut butter and jelly, spinach and oat milk vegan smoothies. You get the point.

I am a faithful companion of 21 years, but I do believe it's perfectly acceptable to date your coworkers. I encourage it! Think about it. Throughout the week who do you spend the majority of your time with, especially if you're in the field of education? It's only natural to become close to your colleagues as you lean on them for help, collaborate, problem-solve, inspire, and lend a shoulder to cry on or provide a safe space and unjudging ear to vent to. Coworkers become a constant in our lives, as they should. For this reason, why shouldn't we be allowed to get a little closer?

I understand that many educators, and their spouses, disagree with my point of view. That's fine; those aren't the ones I want to date when I'm away from home, educating our youth, and creating world changers. They can stay in their monogamous schools.

If you are going to be working with me, in our building, be prepared. You are going to get to know all of our staff very well. You'll build stronger connections with some, but you will have a chance to date everyone if you choose at one point or another throughout the year. If you've ever watched "Bachelor in Paradise," it's kind of like that...on steroids.

One way that I like to get the relationships flowing is by Speed Dating. We'll do this at the beginning of the school year before everyone has loosened up. This is the point of the year where we have some new staff and many still have their walls up even if they've been a part of the team for years. Speed dating early in the school year lets everyone get their uncertainties out right away, learning a little about everyone, especially the rookies, and if anything has changed in the lives of our veterans.

I promote our Speed Dating event via our weekly newsletter, approximately two weeks before our scheduled meeting date. Our weekly newsletter isn't bullet points in an email body. Instead, it legitimately looks like a newspaper with pictures, sections, and headlines. In the upper right-hand corner was the Speed-Dating announcement:

SPEED DATING

We will be Speed Dating at approximately 2:37 on Wednesday, September 12. Please dress to impress. You never know who you'll have a connection with. Love is in the air!

The next few weeks were fun...for me! I had staff coming up and asking all kinds of questions! I knew their minds were spinning, pondering how and why in the world we'd be doing Speed Dating at our first official staff meeting of the year.

"Mike, uuuummm....what is Speed Dating?"

"So, you know we have way more female staff than males right?"

"I've been looking for someone, but I don't think I'm going to find them here."

"Does the Superintendent know what you're doing? More importantly, does your wife know?"

A little background on our district. We have five buildings. Each principal sends a copy of their weekly staff newsletters not only to their respective staff but also to our district leadership team. We also get together monthly, a few days before our staff meeting dates, just to clarify, finalize, vent, and go through stuff principals do when they get together behind closed doors. If you're a building principal, you know what I'm talking about.

Our district principals' meeting was in full effect. We went through all of our agenda items. The last topic, faculty meetings. I sat there, waiting to hear what everyone else had planned. They all went through how they were going to deliver information, build community, and get the year rolling. Now it was my turn to share.

"We're going to be Speed Dating!" is all I said, in a monotone, boring voice.

One of my colleagues replied, "Yeah, I saw that in your newsletter. What is that about?"

"Yeah, what are you doing?" was another question fired at me.

Not only were our staff apprehensive about this uncomfortable activity, but I also had my administrative peers wondering what on Earth I was up to for our next faculty meeting!

After weeks of waiting, like staring at an egg, waiting for a beak to begin cracking through, the day was here! Our staff would finally get to date and know their co-workers a little closer than they ever dreamed! I went to our LRC (Learning Resource Center) about 30 minutes before the student dismissal bell rang. I took our eight rectangle tables and placed them into two rows of 5, placing the rolling chairs on each side to ensure the staff would be facing each other in each row.

After the students were dismissed to enjoy their beautiful Fall afternoon, staff began slowly entering our dating room with apprehension. The lights were dimmed to help set a romantic mood and Marvin Gaye's "Let's Get It On" whispered sweet nothings into the ears of all on repeat. After making a final announcement that our meeting would be starting, I made my way.

I donned my final piece of clothing for the meeting. Took a deep breath into my belly, formed my best Love Connection host smile, and broke through the threshold of the room wearing a magnet with yellow chicks on it draped around my neck. I was greeted with smiles, laughter, and flashes from phone cameras.

With my arms outstretched in front of me, "All right, are we ready to find love?"

I put a timer on the board for 120 seconds.

"Before we begin, I need everyone to take out the article you chose to read for today's meeting."

In the staff newsletter that was sent out the week before the announcement of Speed Dating, I had asked the staff to find an educational article online. This article could have been about any issue in education today. The choice was theirs. Some found articles regarding recess, others RTI. Many had articles that discussed math and reading strategies. The topic wasn't what was important. I wanted staff to read an educational piece of something that they could connect with. If I had assigned the topic, this would more than likely not have happened.

"You are going to have 120 seconds, that's 60 seconds each if you choose, to discuss your article with your current 'date.' After the timer goes off, everyone sitting on the inside rows will move one chair down towards the SmartBoard. If you're on the end, you'll go to the opposite end. Does everyone understand?" I asked as I then scanned the room, making sure to lock eyes with every potential suitor and future couple.

A unanimous, "YES!" filled the joyous air.

"All right, let's find some love!" I shouted and began the time for our first round of dates.

We went through about six rotations.

After these rotations, I asked, "Who made a connection? Is there someone that you enjoyed spending time with today? Please tell us about them and what they had to offer."

At this point, staff began sharing articles that they learned about from their dates. Nobody spoke on their own article that they brought for the day.

"I want to thank everyone for taking a chance at love today. If there is anyone that you made a strong connection with, I encourage you to continue connecting and learning with them after we leave here today," was how I concluded our Speed Dating activity.

Many of our staff continued conversations about articles that sparked their interest on our school-wide Microsoft Teams page. We were also able to post links to every article that was brought forth, creating a library for all staff to learn from if they were unable to get a "date" with that individual at our staff meeting.

My goal was to build anticipation and take a fun approach to sharing educational articles, an activity that every school staff has done before and will again in the future, only I put an engaging spin on it to avoid drudgery. Meaningful conversations were had. Staff had buy-in as to what they were discussing because they had a choice as to what they could research and read. Had everyone read the same assigned article, we would have had a handful or two not even reading it on their own, knowing peers would just fill them in. Also, our staff was able to learn of some passions and interests of their colleagues based on the topic of the article they chose to share.

Peer-to-peer sharing, collaboration, and learning all took place during our Speed Dating activity. It also helped to build relationships with others that they may not normally talk with. In our school, we are all in for every child. There are no "my kids"; these are "our kids."

I am so glad to see our staff break down the walls and rely on each other. Speed Dating has helped us accomplish this. It's not uncommon to see a 5th-grade teacher reaching out to a kindergarten teacher to problem solve, or a 3rd-grade teacher collaborating with a Special's teacher for an activity. Speed Dating has helped us all become comfortable in our strengths and accepting of our weaknesses. We can drop our egos and rely on others across the school from us. This has helped to create an all-in mentality when creating world changers in our students.

Don't worry babe, I'm still coming home to you and only you. I'm looking forward to another 12 years, and then 12 more after that, and another 12, and, well, you get the point. But once every 365 days, I'll put on that Chick Magnet and watch our staff search for love!

SPICY SPEED DATING SOUP

INGREDIENTS

1. Email or messaging system
2. Instructions to research and read an educational article
3. 8 Rectangle tables that seat 4
4. Open space such as library
5. Seats for each participant
6. Sound system/speakers
7. Marvin Gaye's "Let's Get it On" on repeat
8. Stopwatch/timer

PREP TIME

- Prep Time - 21 days
- Cook Time - 15 minutes
- Total Time - 21 days, 15 minutes
- Total Cost - $0

PROCEDURE

1. Approximately 3 weeks out from activity, email participants asking to research and read an educational article of their choosing.
2. Approximately 2 weeks out from activity, email participants that they will be Speed Dating on specific date.
3. 30 minutes prior to activity, go to designated meeting area and arrange rectangle tables in 2 rows of 4.
4. Place chairs facing each other on each side of the tables.
5. Play Marvin Gaye's "Let's Get it On" on repeat over the sound system.
6. Instruct participants they will have 60 seconds to share and summarize their article with the person across from them.
7. After 60 seconds, the inner seats move down a seat to the right.
8. Reset the timer and have the new "dates" repeat Step 6.
9. After 6 rounds or so, have individuals share what article summary had the biggest impact on them and why they would like to learn more about that topic.
10. Share links to each article on a shared document for all participants to view at a later time.
11. Optional - Chick magnet costume.

Speed Dating
By Suzie Henderson
@Suzie_Henderson
Principal

I was just coming off of a very relaxing Christmas break. I was gearing up for the second half of the school year by preparing for our upcoming teacher planning day. I was standing at my desk with my head in my hands drumming my fingers while I was trying to think of a way to shake up our usually dull, sit-and-get meeting. I just knew I couldn't have the usual gathering where we had breakfast and then I fed them information that they could just read in an email. What we needed was time to connect, truly connect with one another. I knew that was an essential piece that we were missing in our staff meetings.

Suddenly I remembered reading a blog by my friend Mike Earnshaw where he talked about an activity he had done with his staff that he called Struggle Island.

Time out...

Mike and I connected through Twitter. I can't remember how long we have been connected or exactly how we got connected, but I am so thankful for this connection. One of the most important lessons I have learned as an administrator is that it is absolutely necessary to stay connected in order to keep growing. The lessons I have learned through my connections are too many to count.

Okay...now back to my story.

After I read Mike's blog, I sent him a voice message in Voxer telling him how much I loved the Struggle Island idea because I had been looking for ideas to enhance our faculty meetings. He sent me a vox back and shared more information about the

Struggle Island activity as well as some other activities he had done with his staff. One of the activities he told me about was Speed Dating.

Ah...Speed Dating. That rang a bell to me because it is a professional learning tool used often by my good friend Mark Wilson. I couldn't wait to hear more. Mike shared with me how he had used it in the past. I filed this away for safe-keeping.

So on that final day of the year, I knew exactly who could help me come up with a great idea for my staff meeting, so I sent Mike a vox telling him what I needed for my staff. I described to him what usually happens on our day back and how I needed to do something different.

Mike shared with me an activity he was going to do with his staff that involved them reflecting on 2019, setting goals for 2020, and finding someone they could help support to reach their goal. I loved this idea so I took it and after a few iterations, I was ready for our first meeting of 2020.

January 6, 2020 began with a quick breakfast and then I let them know what we would be doing.

"I am giving each of you a Reflect and Renew card. On this card I want you to take a few minutes to reflect on 2019 and write goals for 2020. For the Reflect activity, please list what you are most proud of both in your personal life and your educational life. For the Renew activity, please come up with a personal and an educational goal. I also want you to envision what you want for your classroom for the remainder of this school year. Once you finish writing, I am going to put you into 4 groups. Each group will have equal numbers and you will be standing across from someone. I want each person to take a minute to read what is on your card. Your partner will then read what is on their card. When you hear the music start, the person in line on the left will move between the groups to go to the end and everyone in the line on the left will shift to their left. You should get to connect with 5 others before time is up. It is very important that as you listen to one another that you truly comprehend the goals being shared. This will enable you to identify those you can support in the next few months. I will share everyone's goals and you will have opportunities to check in with others. Then in May, we will have a final check in to see how we are all doing. It is so important that we stay connected and support one another."

Just as Mike suggested, I decided to just facilitate rather than take part. I watched as each staff member took their turn to share from their Reflect and Renew card. I listened in on several conversations and learned some things about my staff I didn't know. I learned that one of our paraprofessionals wanted to save money so she could go back to school to be a teacher. Several staff members spoke of wanting to bring more balance to their lives, work out more, eat better, dance and laugh more.

As I listened in, I was able to take pictures and a few videos to capture the moment. I wanted this to be the first of many such connecting moments with my staff.

Thinking about where we are at the time I am writing this, I am so thankful we had that time to connect as I feel it prepared us for what was ahead. Because of the sudden exit from school, we didn't get a chance to circle back to our goals in May, but I am hoping to bring those goals out again before we do this activity. I am so thankful that Mike has been diligent to create and document the different activities he has done with his staff.

One other thing Mike told me has really stuck with me as far as one of the purposes for changing up how we do faculty meetings. This is so important for us as leaders because we often get what we model. He said,

"I want these activities to be able to be taken by the staff who participate in them to use them in their classroom somehow."

If you have not changed up how you do your staff meetings, let my story encourage you to step out of your comfort zone and try something new. Reach out to others who have traveled this road before you. Mike is a good one to connect with. Start small and be amazed at what unfolds when you shake things up a bit. Model for your staff what you want to see in their classrooms: engaged students who are learning not only academics, but how to connect with others in meaningful ways.

REFLECT and RENEW
January 6, 2020

What were you most proud of in 2019?

Personal

Educational

What are your goals for 2020?

Personal

Educational

What do you envision for your classroom for the rest of this school year?

5

STRUGGLE ISLAND STEW

I stared at the illuminated document displayed on my screen, seven items listed, yet my eyes fixated only on #3, Struggle Island. A sinister smile overtook my face and that inner voice let out his best impersonation of the laugh from Mr. Burns, Homer Simpson's infamous, evil, money hungry boss from the hit show, "The Simpsons." I awoke my email app, attached the document as a live link with a faux paperclip, and punched "Send." Now the waiting. This would be the longest three days, but the anticipation would be well worth it.

I couldn't even keep track of how many staff members came up to me over the next 72 hours, all asking the same questions.

"What is Struggle Island?"

"What are we doing with Struggle Island?"

"Do I need to know anything?"

"What should I bring?"

"I can't wait for this faculty meeting!"

That's right. I had our staff salivating at the thought of our next faculty meeting. In other schools across our great nation, many principals spend one hour a month after school with their staff reciting bullet points on a PowerPoint behind them. Many, if not all of these bullets, could easily be sent in an email or newsletter without any verbal explanation and I guarantee that the professional staff they oversee would understand what the directives were. I do things differently. I know I don't want to sit and just read facts to our staff after a long day inspiring our kids, so why in the world would our staff want that either?

"You shouldn't have to worry too much. I would just make sure you're comfortable, make sure to get a good night's rest and eat healthy. I'd suggest working out or getting a run in that morning, but don't overdo it. You don't want to be exhausted," was my reply. Then I creepily stared at them, with that sinister smile contorting my face.

We are constantly telling our teachers that long gone are the days when students sat in straight rows, writing rote notes from what the teacher produced on the board at the front of the room, reciting the same information students could read for themselves. Today's classrooms need to be engaging. Teachers need to build anticipation and excitement into their lessons to have our students bursting back through our doors each day. Today's lessons need to include collaboration, problem-solving, higher-level thinking, engagement, and fun. All of those are ingredients to a mouthwatering lesson. If you don't believe me, go read *Teach Like a Pirate* (2012) by Dave Burgess. Or better yet, go see him keynote or present and tell me you don't think fun, engagement, and anticipation have a place in a successful lesson.

I don't expect our teachers to bring bland, antiquated lessons to their students, so why should I? No educator is excited to stay an hour or two after school when they're exhausted. As principals, our staff meetings are our classrooms; it is our time to engage, inspire, and motivate our staff. It is a time to get our staff collaborating and problem-solving to bring the best, life-changing education to our students. That will not happen by them listening to me drone on through a PowerPoint. As leaders, we need to bring our passions and model the style of lessons we expect our staff to bring to our students.

After going through the first standard items on our agenda, such as the passing of the Gracious Grizzly and 1st grade presenting on how to implement Bead Counters, we arrived at item #3!

The room grew silent as if someone hit the "Mute" button in the room. All eyes made their way to me. I heard Mr. Burns' maniacal laughter echoing in my head. That sinister smile overtook, I gasped a deep breath, then exhaled slowly. Seconds felt like eons. I closed my eyes, placed my shaky hands on the desk in front of me for support. I tilted my head towards the ground and closed my eyes.

"Ok. It's time we go to Struggle Island. You're not going to need to bring anything with you. Your belongings will be safe here, if you're lucky enough to return. If you don't make it back we'll be splitting up amongst ourselves what was left behind, unless you labeled everything or have a will. Unfortunately, there's no time to get it together now. Is everyone ready?"

I made sure to wait with the standard "Pause Time" we expect our teachers to practice when asking a question to their class. I glazed over my audience. Many smiles were filling the room surprisingly, some began cracking their knuckles, and others stared at their closest comrade, searching for safety and sending S.O.S. messages via Morse Code with their blinking eyes.

"All right, follow me," were my last words before we landed on Struggle Island.

I slowly walked out of the LRC (Learning Resource Center) and headed to our back playground. The sun was shining on this October afternoon. There was a strong east wind, swirling leaves, and debris across the field that added to the feeling of despair as we prepared our trip to Struggle Island. Before our staff could begin conversing and getting comfortable, I began shouting.

"All right, everyone needs to form a circle, a nice tight circle. You want to be close enough to hold the person next to you's hand. You don't have to, but you may want to. You have ten seconds to form this circle."

Without speaking, our staff formed their circle. As I scanned the perimeter of their circle, a few were holding hands.

"Welcome to Struggle Island!" I shouted with both of my arms outstretched to the Heavens. From the bullseye of the circle, I declared, "Right now we are all safe!"

"If you remember, two weeks ago I had asked everyone to come to the front office and anonymously fill out an index card with an issue you are facing in the classroom. You then placed them in this manila envelope." I held up the envelope as high as my right arm would allow.

"Inside here are all of our struggles. What I am going to do is remove a card, one at a time, and read it aloud. If you are facing that same struggle, you are to take two steps backward. When you do that, you are now in the murky, shark-infested waters, with no idea of how to get out. If you did not take two steps backward, you are safe on the island. If you are safe on the island, that either means you have never encountered this struggle, or you have a solution to it. If you are still safe on the island, I ask that you throw a lifesaver to your colleagues and share what has worked for you or ideas on how they can find a way out of their struggle."

Two weeks before, so our staff could not put two and two together, I asked in an email for them to come to the office and write a problem they were facing and needed help with. I wanted it anonymous to get true problems that maybe they would normally be afraid to admit they were struggling with. This helped to build anticipation as to why they were doing this. They had no inkling as to why I was asking for this. Then, about two weeks later, I sent the agenda with item #3 only stating, Struggle Island. As far as I know, nobody made the connection.

I had received much positive praise from staff after this activity. It helped to drop the facade that everyone is perfect. Many staff also saw many of their colleagues in a new light, building a strong bond and camaraderie with the vulnerability many shared and helped with that afternoon. This activity helped to share that all of us are facing issues we need help with. It helped to tighten the bond that we are all here for each other, and in turn, our students.

All of us, no matter our years of experience or title, face struggles. We all encounter obstacles that are way too daunting to get around on our own. **We need to drop our egos and ask for help.** Many of our answers are down the hall from our own offices and classrooms. If they're not, reach out on social media. There are so many connected educators that your solution is out there. You are not alone. To be the best, not perfect, but the best for our kids, ask for help. We're here for you.

STRUGGLE ISLAND STEW

INGREDIENTS

1. Large Index Cards
2. Pen
3. Manilla Envelope
4. Secured & Private location to collect cards
5. Email or messaging system
6. Blacktop or open gym floor

PREP TIME

- Prep Time - 21 days
- Cook Time - 30 minutes
- Total Time - 21 days, 35 minutes
- Total Cost - $16 (or $0 if you "borrow" materials from the front office)

PROCEDURE

1. Email or message staff 21 days prior to staff meeting to think of a struggle they are facing in their classroom or education.
2. Email staff 18 days prior to staff meeting to come to the secured location during their "free" time.
3. When staff visit secured location, they are to pick up an index card provided and write a struggle they are facing in their classroom or education.
4. Staff are to place their index card, without their name written on it, in the provided manilla envelope.
5. 7 days prior to staff meeting, send an email or newsletter to staff preparing them that they will be visiting Struggle Island at the next staff meeting.
6. 6. 2 days prior to staff meeting send meeting agenda to staff, listing Struggle Island as the final agenda item.
7. Hold staff meeting in a separate location of where Struggle Island activity will take place.
8. After meeting agenda items are concluded, have staff travel to Struggle Island area.
9. Ask staff to form a circle.
10. State directions of the Struggle Island activity:
    a. A question will be read aloud.
    b. If individuals have solutions to the struggle read out loud, they are to remain where they are, signifying being "safe on the island."
    c. If an individual is facing the same struggle they are to step backwards, out of the circle. This signifies them "drowning in the waters."
    d. Individuals still on the "Island" are to then share what solutions have worked for them to save those "drowning."
11. Go through as many "struggles" as time allows. For those that aren't read, email them out to staff or better yet, list them on a community board, such as Microsoft Teams or Google Classroom.

Smelling Salts
By Jennifer Osman
@jenniferosman4
Teacher

I am embarking in my 18th year in education and that, in part, is because of Mike Earnshaw and his passion as a leader, not only for our students, but for the staff of Oak Glen Elementary.

When I met Mike Earnshaw, I was at a crossroads in my career. My passion was strong, yet my morale was struggling, due to experiences with apathetic school culture and lack of support. School community and culture is, to me, one of the most critical factors in teacher growth and efficacy.

I can, with great appreciation say that I LOVE coming to "work" each day because of the community and culture that Mike creates and fosters at Oak Glen Elementary. Mike puts relationships first; it is evident in his actions and words that he is truly invested in each member of his staff, not only as an educator but as a person. I feel supported and encouraged to take risks with my students in pursuit of just the right fit for all students. There is rarely a day that goes by that I do not see Mike in the hallways interacting with students or staff or stopping in my own classroom to check out and share in something new I am trying. I welcome any feedback from my principal because he actually has a clue about my goals and philosophies as an educator.

Mike Earnshaw leads by example in his interactions with students; his passion is contagious. I am grateful to work with a leader who puts so much effort into identifying the ingredients he uses to create the recipes found in this book for a healthy school community and culture. I know that the ideas and concepts found in the content of these pages will find the reader inspired to create and foster this same community and culture in their own environment.

6

LITERATURE-O-LANTERNS LASAGNA

While staff meetings are a crucial time for administrators to inspire, motivate, problem-solve, and get faculty collaborating on issues facing their school, classrooms, and students, sometimes we just need to have fun! Not every minute of every staff meeting needs to be filled with data-driven analysis and initiatives.

October is a month where the "Honeymoon" phase has ended for many. Educators are now in the thick of school. While building meaningful, impactful, loving relationships is an ongoing process, the "Get to Know You" activities that are completed in the first few weeks of school are over. True personalities from not only the students, but staff as well, have been revealed. The review material that is covered from the students' previous grade level is now complete and teachers have a better picture of their students' academic state.

I've been in the game of education for nearly 20 years. I'm not a math teacher nor do I ever do countdowns, so I have no idea how long I have "officially" been an educator for or how many years I have left to retire. I'm enjoying my role and those numbers don't mean anything to me. But throughout this time, I have learned that October staff meetings are typically the ones that if they are not planned out properly can turn into a complaining session faster than the weather changes throughout a Fall day in Chicago.

October is a great month to bring in activities that focus solely on creativity, community, and sharing. This is true not only for faculty at a staff meeting but for our students as well. Everyone needs time to disengage from the rigor of the game, staff, and students. We all need Brain Breaks to not overwork our strongest muscle. We all need to just enjoy the company with others, sharing stories and laughter as they show off their interests and creativity.

Enter Literature-O-Lanterns. I had first learned about this activity while attending a conference. Two amazing presenters, Dr. Andy Jacks and Lindsay Stumpenhorst, were presenting on interacting with your staff. They shared many great activities that lend themselves to collaboration and problem solving, but then Dr. Jacks said something that resonated with me.

"Sometimes, you just need to have fun."

Inside, my inner voice, the much smarter me, shouted, "That's it! This is perfect for October!"

I left that breakout session knowing that October's staff meeting had the best finisher, Literature-O-Lanterns. It was hard to keep this activity a secret for the next three months. It became extremely hard once we completed September's staff meeting. The next day I was bombarded by falling missiles, questions from staff, from every direction when skateboarding through the halls.

"So, yesterday's meeting was awesome! What are we doing for October?"

"Is October's meeting going to be as fun? I got a lot out of yesterday's activity."

"You think you can top yesterday? I'm excited for our next meeting. Is that weird?"

I felt like the best friend of a girl that knew her boyfriend was going to be getting down on one knee and asking her to commit the rest of her life to creating a beautiful life with him. I had to bite my lip each time I was asked about October's meeting to keep my smile from drifting off of my face like a professional race car taking a turn much too quickly.

"I have some ideas, it should be fun. I'll get some info out soon," was my bland office manager reply.

I knew what I had to do. The recipe called for strategic dissemination of ingredients that were needed for the staff to bring. We had roughly 20 days before our October meeting. That was about three staff newsletters that would be sent out before it. I figured the first piece of bait would be dropped immediately in the following week's newsletter. This would give me enough time to wait until not the following, but the final newsletter was delivered to everyone's inbox so that hopefully, they couldn't put the recipe together before the dinner date.

I began building the anticipation for our October staff meeting slowly, much like the first time a child attempts to build a house of cards. The only difference was that I was determined to not let my house fall anytime before we met.

In the section of our newsletter focusing on the upcoming staff meeting, I simply posted the date of the meeting as a reminder. All staff have already been given the calendar and were instructed to ensure they would not have any outside commitments throughout the year that interfere with our meetings. Besides the date, the only information I provided was to bring a copy of your favorite children's or young adult piece of literature and not to tell anyone what it is.

Like a programmed DVR knows its schedule, I knew what was about to happen while I rolled through our hallways and crossed through the thresholds of the classrooms that contained magic.

"Ok, so does it matter what book we bring?"

I was asked this basic question in about 247 different word variations. I stayed consistent in my response, "What did the newsletter say? Bring a copy of your favorite children's or young-adult book. If it's a kid's book, you can't go wrong. But don't tell anyone!"

There was always a follow-up. "So, can I bring (insert every child or young adult piece of literature you can imagine here)?"

The Mike inside me would let out a big sigh, and then I would reply, "If that's a kid's book yep! But make sure you keep it a secret!"

Nine school days had passed. In October; that's the equivalent of 27 for some. They're left scratching their heads not understanding how it's still the same month. It was time for another newsletter. It was time for me to drop another ingredient into their laps, wishful thinking that nobody was able to mix the two prematurely.

In our newsletter which was now seven school days away from our meeting, I wrote another update. The previous weeks were just a repeat of our original announcement of kids' literature. This time, it included that, but at the end, I added a little P.S. Like when you want to throw in that cute little love note to your crush or significant other to make them think you just remembered something special about them, but in reality the entire premise behind your note, email or text was just to tell them the P.S.

"Please bring a medium-sized pumpkin to the meeting."

You guessed it, questions galore.

"Why do we need a pumpkin?"

"Are we carving pumpkins?"

"What is this for? Do we really need to bring a pumpkin?"

"Yes, you need a pumpkin. It's part of our staff meeting and you won't be able to participate if you don't have one. I've got two kids, I can't buy any extras, it's a struggle to get one for myself!" That's what I pretty much told everyone that questioned the pumpkin request.

Literature-O-Lanterns Lasagna

The morning of the meeting I was approached by two of our Special's teachers. Both of them teach art to varying grade levels.

"Hey Mike, do you need anything special today with the pumpkins?" they asked in unison.

I responded with hesitation, "Well, I could use some help, but I don't want to spoil the surprise of what we're doing for anyone. That includes you two."

Both of these amazing educators looked me in the eyes and said, "We won't tell anyone what's going on. Let us know how we can help. With the pumpkins, we just feel it's going to get messy."

I talked to myself in my head for a few moments before responding. My inner-Michael was telling me to just let them help, but I was apprehensive. After what felt like minutes, I responded.

"All right, here's what we're doing." I proceeded to tell them my plan of what our staff would be completing with the pumpkins they brought in. "So it would be better if you were able to set everything up for that in here, the Art Room. You'd be able to do that?" I questioned like a little boy asking his mother for that item on the store shelf he so desperately thinks he needs.

Both of their eyes widened, mouths gaped open, then they responded, "That's a great activity! Let us help you! It'll be so much better here. We can do this!"

I was sold. I knew that by dropping the facade of me doing everything myself, I would be able to do this activity more justice. I trusted these two, and I also knew that by having the staff move from our meeting area in the LRC to the Art Room would allow for much-needed movement breaks, curiosity as to where and why we were moving, and a fresh learning environment. Not all learning needs to, nor should, take place within your four classroom walls.

Literature-O-Lanterns was the concluding item on our agenda. It was very difficult to get through the first items, like sprinting through quicksand. Once we made it to the end, it was well worth it.

"All right, I see everyone has their pumpkin and book, that's great! Thanks for following directions!" I said with a smile. "While I have everyone's attention, I'm going to give you the instructions now. When I say, we're going to head to the Art Room, all you need to bring is your pumpkin and book. Once there, you'll take a seat and begin painting your pumpkin to represent your favorite book!"

Someone in the back of the room shouted out, "What else?"

With my arms raised above my head, I said, "That's it! We're going to paint our pumpkins and then have them on display in the LRC."

At this point, many began to quietly talk with their neighbors, smiles covering their faces, an aroma of excitement permeated throughout the air.

"All right, let's go!"

The vibe in the Art room was amazing! Cooperation, discussion, encouragement, and laughter were abounding! Everyone proudly worked on their Literature-O-Lanterns and chatted about school, home life, and amazement at some of the artistic talent their colleagues had been keeping a secret.

"You know what we should do?" someone at the middle table shouted. The room immediately grew silent, all eyes and ears were on our speaker. "We should put cards next to each pumpkin and have the students guess who designed which one."

A wave of "Yes!" flowed through the room.

"Perfect, let's make it happen!" was what I said as everyone went back to their rough, uneven canvas.

For the next week or two, all of our Literature-O-Lanterns were on display in the LRC. Saying the students loved seeing them as they entered is an understatement. The kids had a blast admiring the hard work put into each one, guessing to see which book it represented, and then challenging each other to determine who the artist behind each one was.

Our LRC clerk said that within the first thirty minutes of school, students were bursting through the doors, politely and appropriately, of course, to see what the hype was their peers were raving about. Over the next few weeks, she had more students visiting the LRC to admire the temporary art display, and in return, had more students checking out books and READING!

Literature-O-Lanterns served multiple purposes that affected everyone in our school.

1. The anticipation of the activity had buy-in and eagerness from our staff. They were looking forward to our monthly staff meeting, something usually unheard of in many schools.
2. The activity itself brought about community, collaboration, and camaraderie. Expressing creativity, sharing supplies, and engaging in appropriate small talk amongst peers are skills and expectations we have for our students. This helped our educators see what it's like.
3. Each educator was able to showcase a little bit about themselves. It helped to open themselves up to others by showing their book of choice and their artistic abilities. Not only did the staff learn more about their peers, the students learned more about the adults that are in their lives every day.
4. By having students eager to visit the LRC to see and learn about their teachers, they were checking out more books and

reading more, just because they had a reason to get into the LRC! More reading is never a bad thing.
5. A few teachers took this activity and incorporated a version of it in their classrooms with their students.

Not every activity that takes place in school needs to be tied to a specific standard or address a deficit area. Not every focus needs to be analyzing data, addressing test scores, and looking for ways to improve them. Sometimes, the best approach is to build a little community and have some fun being with each other. Sharing laughs, getting creative, and just spending time with one another as people will help to shift a school's culture towards more positivity, collaboration, and success.

LITERATURE-O-LANTERN LASAGNA

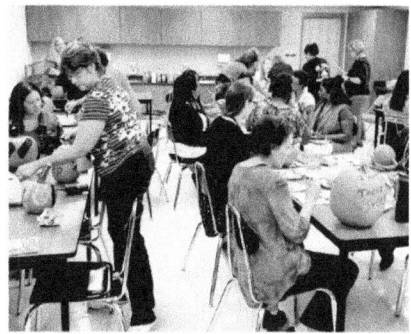

INGREDIENTS

1. Email or messaging system
2. Pumpkin - Medium-sized
3. Children's/Young Adult Book
4. Paint
5. Paintbrushes
6. Water
7. Paper Towels
8. Collaborative learning area with tables and room to move

PREP TIME

- Prep Time - 7 days
- Cook Time - 30 minutes
- Total Time - 7 days, 30 minutes
- Total Cost - $15

PROCEDURE

1. Email participants they need to bring a medium-sized pumpkin to the activity date.
2. Email participants, in a separate email from Step 1, that they need to bring their favorite children's/young adult book to the activity date.
3. 1 hour before the meeting, set up a separate location with tables, paint, paintbrushes, and water for cleaning.
4. Do not make mention of the pumpkins or books at all during the meeting.
5. When approximately 35 minutes are remaining of the meeting, instruct participants they will bring their pumpkins and book to the separate location. At this location, they will paint a representation of their book on their pumpkin.
6. Let pumpkins dry on a shelf overnight.
7. The next morning move all pumpkins to an area where students, staff, and visitors can see them on display.
8. Optional - voting and/or guessing the artist or book representation challenges.

Social-Emotional Staff Meetings
By Dr. Andy Jacks
@_AndyJacks
Principal

Leaders have a great influence on how our staff feels after our meetings. For a long time, I overlooked the importance of the social-emotional well-being of the staff and how much our meetings helped or at times hurt them. When we focus so much on academic instruction and old-school professional development, we often miss the larger picture of our roles as leaders. Trust. Relationships. Motivation. These are critical elements to consider when planning for meetings. Staff meetings are our time as leaders to be role models for learning, to inspire staff to want to achieve more with their students, and to build relationships. One successful strategy we use is to add field trips, projects, and hands-on activities. We try to remove the mundane and menial routines from the agenda and give more time for what really matters. Time for positive adult social interactions. Time for fun. If staff feel worse after our meetings, that's on us. We can do better. But we'll need to totally rethink the purpose of our time together. Let's take the pressure off ourselves to teach them how to do everything in their jobs. We don't have enough time or the ability to do that anyways. Make them feel good. Give them an EXPERIENCE. Plan something they will laugh about during the activity and talk about afterward. Connect the activity to a higher purpose, goal, or analogy, so we can be better for each other and for our students. Just like our students, we want our staff to run into our school and our meetings, not out of them!

7

WEAKNESS WAFFLES

"I don't like numbers, I never taught math, I was an English teacher."

As you can see from my statement above, I can't even count how many times I have had these words escape my mouth or some version of them. I've never been a fan of data analysis, simply because I don't understand it.

Throughout my years in education, I have come to the point where I will admit this. I have stated my dislike of data analysis and lack of comprehending it in front of my staff and district office administrators. During my evaluation, before my Superintendent and Director of Curriculum and Assessment could explain, with evidence, how I lack at comprehending data, I pointed it out myself.

"Look, I know I am weak when it comes to data. That is something I need to work on, and want to get better with. I'm not comfortable with it but am setting a goal to get better with it. I'm a great cheerleader, a motivator, and leader, but the piece I'm missing is data," was what I said before they could go into my evaluation and rankings.

"We're glad you admit that, and yes, that is something we would like you to work on. You have the culture piece down, you are very good at that, and with a bump in understanding data you will be an extremely effective leader, covering all areas," was their response.

For a school year, I exited my comfort zone when it came to my evaluation. There are three components administrators are evaluated on: student growth, a professional goal, and an organizational goal. While student growth is primarily set by the district office, we do have a little say in what our goal growth percentages will be. The professional and organizational goals are mainly the administrator's choice.

When an individual gets to choose their own goal to be evaluated on, many will stay safe in their comfort zone.

"So are you going to focus on culture and staff meetings? You can set a goal for expanding professional development. You already have some of it covered with how you send book summaries to the District Leadership Team every week," was a recommendation posed by a fellow principal.

"I don't know, I could, I mean, I am pretty good at that. But I feel it's already established," was my response.

"But that'll make it easier and you won't have to worry about not making it. That's what I would do if I were you," was what they then shared as their last two cents.

"So what are you thinking for your professional goal, Mike?" my Superintendent inquired.

"I'm thinking I want to focus on data. I'm weak in that area and by not putting myself on the line, stepping out of my comfort zone, and doing what I preach to my staff daily, is the only way I will get better at it. So working with my staff on understanding, analyzing, and discussing data is my professional goal," was my definitive response.

My Superintendent and Director of Curriculum and Assessment glanced at each other and without muttering a word, knew they agreed with what I stated my professional goal would be.

I broke the silence. "I just don't know how we want to measure it."

"We can track how you discuss and analyze data with your staff. How does that sound?" my Superintendent suggested

I had the wheels spinning in my mind. "All right, but I don't want any numbers attached to this goal. This goal needs to evaluate how I am discussing data more frequently with my staff. Student growth focuses on actual growth; this is just that I'm analyzing, discussing, and becoming more comfortable with data. I'm not going to shoot myself in the foot by attaching a specific number of students that meet a target with this."

"Ok, that's fair, we can work with that," was his response after a nonverbal conversation with my Director of Curriculum and Assessment.

Together, the three of us created my goal. I would be discussing our local assessment data with my Team Leaders. Here's a breakdown of what I would need to do to help meet my evaluation goal:

1. I would create a spreadsheet for every homeroom teacher's math and reading rosters.
2. Teachers would need to put in their students' Spring scores from the previous school year and Fall scores from the current school year.
3. After scores are entered, each teacher would determine a "focus group" and highlight them. This group should have students that are right on the cusp of breaking into the next level.
4. Teachers need to distinguish and implement what interventions and strategies they are putting forth in their classrooms to address their focus groups.
5. I would continually meet with Team Leaders monthly to discuss their progress, how their teams are working, and what their hypothesis will become at the Winter assessment window.

6. After the Winter assessment, teachers will log their Winter scores onto the spreadsheet and analyze if their interventions were effective or not based on how their "focus group" students performed.

No numbers are attached. As I said, I don't like numbers. Instead, we're showcasing that I am comfortable with discussing and analyzing data with my Team Leaders.

"All right, so part of my evaluation is based on analyzing and discussing data with staff. That's you. I don't know too much about how to do this effectively. These are my thoughts, what do you think? How can we do this?" was what I asked my Team Leaders one beautiful Autumn morning while we were locked inside a stuffy conference room.

Silence screamed throughout the four white walls. The quiet ricocheted off of the unplugged Promethean Board. Jaws almost hit the faux wood oval conference table and eyes were opened wide without anyone's first cup of coffee being consumed.

I cut through the silence. "Look, I'm not worried. We got this. I need to get better with data, so why not tie it to my evaluation to ensure I don't mess this up."

After that, there were some comments about how it was admirable about my approach. Then, the seven of us got to brainstorming on how we, as a team, could unroll this to the remaining staff members to be not only successful for me and my evaluation, but also to truly have them begin analyzing and getting comfortable with data and the benefits it can bring to their approach to instructing our students.

I have always been open with my staff about my uncomfortableness with analyzing data. When I would have to, as directed by District Office, I sought out a fellow principal in the district to script what I needed to say to sound like I knew what I was talking about. This didn't help me truly learn what was being said by our numbers, nor did the staff buy into the value of data.

By admitting my weakness, by stating as the leader of a school, to my staff that I needed help, I showed vulnerability. This honesty displayed humility. This honesty showcased that I was human.

None of us are perfect. If you are, you wouldn't be reading this book. You wouldn't need any of my advice. To ensure we are successful, and that we need each other to forge through this fight to bring the best education to our students, we must admit our faults and ask for help when we need it.

I declared I needed help and put my job on the line for it. I did this because it was the only way that I could build strength in a weakness that I have. It also helped me to garnish the support of my staff. It showed them that while I am always there to support them and back them up, I needed them to pick me up as well. It showed that I trusted them, and believed in them to help me where I lacked.

I am still no expert in data analysis. But when new assessments are taken and scores are published, I now have more confidence in knowing what I'm looking at. And while I'm analyzing the numbers, it's not uncommon to have someone approach the invisible threshold of my mobile office or have an email pop through saying, "Do you need any help with the data?"

Everyone has areas of strength and areas of growth. We must acknowledge and know these personal thresholds. This is what will help to create unity, the all-in approach schools need to be the best for their students. Where I lack, I can turn to my staff, and vice versa. Students see this humility also. We must admit to them we don't have all the answers, but that is the beauty of education. There is always something more to learn, to experience, and many times we need others to help us get there.

WEAKNESS WAFFLES

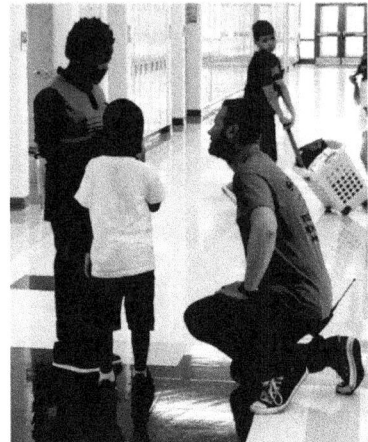

INGREDIENTS

1. Know your strengths
2. Know your weaknesses
3. An ego checked at the door
4. An opportunity to admit a weakness
5. Individuals that have strength where you are weak

PREP TIME

- Prep Time - 39.5 years to drop the ego
- Cook Time - 0.2 seconds
- Total Time - 39.5 years & 0.2 seconds
- Total Cost - $0.0

PROCEDURE

1. Write out a list or journal what your strengths and weaknesses are.
2. Drop the ego and understand that no one is perfect and to succeed in life we MUST rely on others.
3. When opportunities arise to showcase your strengths when others need it, help them.
4. When opportunities arise when you are facing a situation that you need help, seek out those that can, and will help you.
5. Display gratitude and humility to those sharing their strength to teach you and help you succeed.
6. Give credit to others when credit is due.

Just Me
By Kristen Nann
@nankr1120
Educator

The need to reach others should always supersede the desire to **be. all. the. things.** But, maybe that's just me.

Oftentimes I feel as though teachers put on their best face and go after all things in life with such conviction that we push ourselves into a world of perfectionism. A world of untouchable, unrealistic, unattainable perfection. In conversations and through my own experiences, I have been on the end of questions that are looking for my answer to be "the all be it"… "the answer, of all answers"… "the one and only" and why? Well, that hasn't always been nearly as clear to me. Possibly, it comes from us as educators putting pressure on ourselves to be the experts in the field of teaching, masters of all content, a person of vision. Maybe it's a way for us to hold ourselves high and with confidence when delivering what we want others to walk away with as "the answer." No matter how you see it, the real learning comes from a place of honesty. The kind of honesty that confidently speaks knowledge and allows for humility and vulnerability in the form of not knowing and open dialogue.

To be quite honest, it wasn't until after a tragic accident about ten years ago that I realized just how much I was wrapped up in having all the answers all of the time. I had suffered from a fall that ultimately sent me head over feet down a flight of stairs, landing on my concrete basement head first. After suffering from a severe concussion and having to be put to sleep for several days, I woke up without my language base and with the realization, I may not be able to think the same, be a mother to my children, a wife to my husband, let alone teach. What a humbling experience to have my then five-year-old son, Trent, beat me hands-down at round after round of the memory game. How vulner-

able I was to hold my youngest son, Jack, knowing he would now have a new mother caring for him as I was not the same person, in intelligence or personality. After months of intense physical therapy, I was given the go-ahead to enter back into the real world... the classroom. A space that I used to feel so at home in, now felt foreign, cold, and intimidating. I found myself not being able to retrieve information in my own mind and unable to navigate the right path to finding it. I lost materials by the minute and watched my confidence fade away with my future. It was then that I knew the only way to regain my footing was to step out in front of my fears... the one that revealed my faults, my shortcomings, just me. It was then that I became:
Touchable
Relatable
Humanized

I was on a new journey towards empathy and understanding wrapped up in an armful of grace. I found myself saying "how it was" in place of searching for the "right" answer... one that I would probably not retrieve even if I tried. I laughed more at myself so that I could beat others to the moment, but in turn, found my way to lighter humor and a less self-absorbed space of seriousness. I no longer tried to have it all together.... It was too exhausting to even think about let alone attempt. I became real... real with myself and in turn others. I can't help but think this is why I absorb so much around me as I look for the realness in others just the same. Those that are:
Touchable
Relatable
Humanized

The way that others desire to **be. all. the. things, but put others first...** this is more than just me.

8

HANSEL & GRETEL'S CRUMB CAKE

You know how there's that saying when you walk into an area you're not supposed to, like you're not one of the clique, how "The record stops playing"? "All eyes turn to you"? I can remember the first time that I truly experienced this. Believe it or not, it wasn't when I was a punk-rock-skateboarding teen sporting a mohawk held up with Elmer's Glue, size 60-inch balloon-like pants, and faux leather collars (save the animals!) donning spikes around my neck and wrists. No, the moment that I experienced this feeling like an outsider, not welcomed amongst the group, was when I was in my second year as a 7th-grade Assistant Principal.

It was early April. The sun blazing through our windows, having every pre-teen adolescent, and staff member, wishing they were outside. It had been a long winter and even lengthier teacher evaluation season. But, this 8th grade ELA course was inside, studying S.E. Hinton's classic, *The Outsiders*.

Classes had been in session for approximately 240 seconds. I broke the threshold of an 8th-grade ELA class. The teacher, placed in the front of the perfectly symmetrical square classroom by the whiteboard, was finishing her discussion of the day's bell ringer writing prompt. The classroom was split in two: three rows of desks facing north and another three rows of desks facing south. There was a clear path between the two for the teacher to walkabout. It reminded me of comedic cartoon scenes that portrayed the Civil War, North vs. South, facing each other, prepared and salivating for battle, yet neither side placing a toe over the line.

The teacher muzzled her speaking mid-sentence, all student heads shifted robotically towards the doorway, where I stood bearing a smile and laptop. I knew many of the students from the previous school year when they were with me in seventh grade. We said "Hi" without breaking the silence with any words. I quickly scanned the room for an empty seat. Perfect, back row, South Side. I made my way and sat down.

The teacher continued with her wrap-up of the journal, which was connected to the day's discussion of the chapter where Ponyboy and Johnny bleach their hair and then cut it with a dull Swiss Army Knife. My smile never escaped me as I reminisced of the discussions I had with my 8th-graders the 13 years I taught this timeless, classic story.

"Hey Mike, was there a reason you went into that eighth-grade class today?" was the interrogation question I was pummeled with from the 8th-grade Assistant Principal.

I was confused, flabbergasted, not quite knowing why I was being asked this, which felt like an accusation. I didn't feel interrogated by my fellow AP posing the question, but by the teacher.

"Uuumm...what do you mean? Was that a problem?" I responded in a shocked-yet-concerned tone.

My comrade took a sigh and said, "No, she was just wondering if there was a problem. Like why would an administrator that doesn't oversee her grade come into her room for an informal observation."

Ok, I could see the validity in this comment and concern. Up until I moved into the 7th-grade Assistant Principal position, staff was only observed, both formally and informally, by their grade-level AP. Taking time to stop and think before I speak isn't one of my strongest suits, and this conversation was no exception.

"I didn't know that we couldn't visit other grade-level classrooms? I just figured with all of my formal evaluations for seventh grade complete, I wanted to see what was happening in other parts of the school I don't regularly get to see. Also, I heard she's an amazing teacher and I wanted to see her in action. I can say, she did not disappoint!" I responded. Pretty damn good for not gathering my thoughts I must say! Usually, I'll say something and get myself in trouble. I'm slowly learning.

My colleague shook her head, let out another sigh of annoyance, and said, "That's what I told her. She was just very concerned because she's never had another grade level AP come in to observe. I told her I'd ask to make sure."

There is a stigma in our schools that when an administrator enters a room, takes a seat, and opens a notepad, or in today's world a laptop, they are only there for a "gotcha". We've all been there. You're excited for the day, inspiring the minds of your students, putting learning into their own hands. Then somehow, as if you just gained the superpower of hearing better than any feline, your classroom door opens. Standing there, unannounced, is, gasp, an administrator! You haven't seen this individual since the last faculty meeting nearly 14 school days ago! Hopefully, they at least give you a fake smile before taking a seat to follow directions from The Police. Not the local authorities, but The Police, led by Sting. "Every breath you take, every move you make, I'll be watching you."

I've felt this way throughout my tenure as a classroom teacher. If an administrator came in when it wasn't a scheduled formal observation, I always wondered what they were looking for? What was I doing wrong? What are they trying to get "data" on to prove I'm not an effective educator?

These feelings are commonplace in our classrooms, but that doesn't make them acceptable. I know that during my first years as a principal our staff felt the same when I walked in and made myself a comfortable participant in their room, unannounced. This needed to change.

I needed to find a way, a means, to assure our staff that when I entered their room for any reason other than simply to ask them a question, I wasn't there to catch them slipping up. I'm a very tech savvy individual and am not a fan of paper. Every evaluation, whether formal or informal, is completed on my laptop, notes, scripting, and the whole shebang. I knew that I couldn't bring in my laptop for these hangouts which were more for me to build relationships with our students and be a support for our amazing staff. I needed something to leave behind, a little trace, that I notice and appreciate the amazing things that our teachers are doing to change the lives of our students.

I've always loved fairy tales. Even to this day, I enjoy reading them and analyzing all of the different lessons that we can learn to better our lives and positively impact others. During this time while I was trying to find a way to leave my mark and prove that I wasn't in a classroom for evaluation purposes, I thought about the story of Hansel and Gretel. If you're not familiar with the story, I highly suggest you check it out; there's plenty of free versions to read on your own or have read to you on YouTube. I don't care how old or educated you are, everyone loves to be read to. To sum up, Hansel and Gretel's story best ties to my story; our protagonists embark on a journey and leave a trail of breadcrumbs behind them to find their way back home.

"World's best admin assistants?" I said in an excited and rushed voice as I exited my front office one crisp, Autumn morning before students filled our halls and classrooms with smiles and laughter.

I've heard that tone before. They knew I was going to be asking for something I needed for a new project I was ecstatic about. "Yes, Michael?" one replied as she slowly looked up at me from underneath her glasses.

"I need Post-Its. Where do we keep them?" I asked as if time was running out.

"Oh!" the other replied in a "That was easier than I expected from him" tone. "Right here, what kind do you want? What color?"

Without haste, I responded, "The regular square size, colors? Something that sticks out to me, you know I'm color blind. How about pink?"

I went into three classrooms that day. Three classrooms, unannounced. Three classrooms that I did not want to use for any evaluation purposes, informal or formal. Three classrooms that were decided upon from "The Cards." Each classroom I spent a minimum of twenty minutes in. I talked with the students, I completed the activities alongside them, and I gave the teachers' instructions my full attention, modeling what we expect from our students.

I've done all of this before, but each time staff still felt that I was using it for some ulterior motive. This time would be different. This time, I left a breadcrumb behind in each classroom I visited. Before I left each room, I made sure to leave a handwritten note on an extra large Post-It and leave it on the teacher's desk. I can't remember exactly what I wrote on those breadcrumbs, but I can tell you it had nothing but positives on it. Here's an example of what a breadcrumb of mine may say:

Jeannie,

I love how you get to know everything about all of our students. You do a great job of bringing in their passions and interests into your lessons. They know that you truly care for them and their success, yet you are going to push them out of their comfort zone to truly learn what they're capable of. I'm so glad we're on the same team. Keep it up!

- Mike

Leaving breadcrumbs behind in each classroom I visit has become commonplace. I can't remember every positive thing I write, and that's the point. These aren't for me. They are not to be used in an evaluation. These are to let our staff know they are making a difference in our students' lives. To remind them on those days that may feel like the educational world, or maybe even the entire world, is against you. These breadcrumbs are to let our staff know that I notice them, I appreciate them, and I care for the hard work they do.

After leaving breadcrumbs to our staff for an entire year, I didn't know what year two would bring. I did continue them; it is an act that I know I would appreciate. There have been a few instances that I have been called on the radio and had to leave a room before I could rip off my crumb. When that has happened, I've been approached in the halls later, at my mobile office by that staff member.

"Mike, why didn't you leave a note today?" is what I've been questioned about.

I was shocked and befuddled that a teacher, who probably at this point had received at least five breadcrumbs from me, was disappointed to not receive one. "Uuummm….you mean today. I had to run out. I'm sorry."

"Oh, that's all right, I just didn't know if something was wrong," she responded before we shared a laugh.

Ironically, an act I started to use as a non-evaluative practice turned into one once I DIDN'T do it. What truly blew me away though was that I later found out that not only did that staff member, but every staff member kept the notes I had left them. Teachers shared with me that they had them saved in their desk drawers, posted in their personal closet to see every morning where they place their belongings away, and some even posting them on their corkboards behind their desk or taping them on their laptops as reminders of positivity on those days they need them the most.

I'm not sure how many crumbs I've left behind, but I know it will add up to a very delicious cake our staff could share as a celebration.

HANSEL & GRETEL'S CRUMB CAKE

Melanie,
Thank you so much for all you do for OG! You truly have super powers to get it all done. Thanks for making me laugh. You are irreplaceable! Keep changing the game!
—Mike

INGREDIENTS

1. Names of individuals to visit/observe
2. 10 minutes, give or take
3. Post-It Notes
4. Pen

TIME

- Prep Time - 30 seconds
- Cook Time - 10 minutes
- Total Time - 10 minutes, 30 seconds
- Total Cost - $9.99

PROCEDURE

1. Before the day gets started, decide who you will be visiting/observing (sometimes surprise randoms will happen)!
2. Visit/observe the chosen individual for at least 10 minutes.
3. Observe the positive interactions, qualities, & traits displayed by the chosen individual.
4. Before leaving the observation area, write down a personalized note, on the Post-It, referencing the positive attributes.
5. Leave Post-It in a private area, yet observed will find. A personal desk is a great spot!
6. Don't limit yourself to only leaving Post-Its for those you chose that day. Always be on the lookout for positivity & opportunities to leave a note!

The Power of the Post-It
By Jeannie Fry
@jeanniefry158
4th Grade Teacher

In most facets of life, building relationships is key. As an educator, they are essential for the emotional growth and academic success of our students. But what about us? What about teachers as individuals? Principals building relationships with their staff is just as vital. One of the best parts of our current leader is he takes the time to do the little things that make us feel appreciated, and more importantly, valued. Mike has a simple system. Each staff member has an index card with his/her name on it. He pulls two cards a day and those teachers get a visit from him. He sits and observes, interacts with the kids, etc. When the visit is over, Mike always puts a post-it on your desk that praises you for all the things that went great during his time in the classroom. As a staff, we look forward to these small, yet impactful moments. Sometimes, it is just a little post-it that provides the pick me up needed to keep going!

Oh No, Here He Comes!
By Sara Fortin
Kindergarten Teacher

"Oh no....he's coming! I hope he's not coming into my room!" This is the thought most teachers have when they see their principal walking towards them while they are getting ready to teach a lesson. Panic typically sets in and teachers begin stuttering over their words thinking, "Did I just open my lesson, did I state the purpose, am I calling on that student too much/not enough...."

I'm happy to say this has never been my thought when I see Mr. Earnshaw walking, or rather skateboarding, into my room. It's funny how he can have a calming feeling when he comes into the room. It's hard to describe, but the mood shifts in me and my students in a positive way. I know that even though he's coming for an informal observation, I get that feeling of comfort and calmness when he walks in.

I know what it is for my kindergarten students. They love when anyone walks into the room (sorry it's not just you Mr. Earnshaw)! But for myself, I know what's coming. His local legend note. He stays for a while, and upon leaving, he sticks a note to my desk. I have a stack of these notes. I save them for "rainy" days. I reread them when I need some extra encouragement, when I'm questioning my decision on why I'm a teacher. We've all had those thoughts, but most people can't reread a note from their boss and make themself remember why they are in the profession they chose. Mr. Earnshaw has a way with words. He can make you smile with his words of encouragement. He recognizes a hard lesson and writes about what I did to make it a success. Currently, his notes from watching me teach online make it seem like I went to college to teach e-learning.

I feel lucky that I have been given the opportunity to work for such a positive principal. It's funny how a little note left on my desk makes me want to do better, but it certainly does.

9

TEXTING TOAST

"I just wanted to say thank you for helping out last night! It meant a lot to our kids, families, and me! Glad we're on the same team." That's what I Swyped, quickly screened for typos, and punched send.

This text was sent on a Saturday in September at approximately 10:45 AM. We're in Central Time, so I wanted to ensure it wasn't setting off a "Ding" on the recipients too early on a crisp, sun-filled Saturday morning where staff can savor a warm cup of joe. This was the morning educators deserve, grazing out their kitchen window, or even outside on their patio knowing they will finally get to complete their cup of coffee without having to put it down and return to it hours later. I sent this text, individually, to four staff members of our school. Why you ask? The night prior was our PTA sponsored "Back to School Bash!" We had a brand-spankin' new PTA Board this school year and they were doing things a little differently than what our staff, students, and families have ever experienced. In years past, the "Bash" was held indoors. Dancing in the gym, selfie opportunities in the hallway that connected to the MPR (Multi-Purpose Room) which housed games, face painting, pizza, and snacks. This year, this Friday night's "Back to School Bash" was completely outdoors, except for food that was still in the MPR. Outside on the K-2 playground were a plethora of games, a DJ filling the air with today's popular hits as well as those from years past which ignited families to dance, a 50/50 raffle in which one winner wins half of the money raised from selling raffle tickets while the PTA retains the other half, and bounce houses! It was a blast for everyone! Even the Mayor came out to enjoy the festivities! Many of our staff made appearances with their children, but four, the four that I texted this chapter's opening statement to, stayed the entire night and helped to chaperone and work the games on their own accord. No timesheets were turned in, no stipends offered, and no "extra duty" contractual responsibilities were being met.

Why did I send the text? Simple, I wasn't able to tell those four staff members that stayed to help, on their own time and of their own accord, "Thank you!" face-to-face before we left for the night. If you've never stayed until the very end of an after-school event, I highly encourage you to. Chances are if you're reading this cookbook, you've gone above and beyond for our students so this next scene is all too familiar. All of the adults working begin scrambling to clean up and get everything back in order faster than the world's fastest hot dog eater Joey Chestnut at the Nathan's Annual Hot Dog Eating Contest held every Fourth of July. Everyone's fuel levels are on "E" from putting on a great evening event for our students and their families and everyone craves to get home and top the night off with a frosty adult beverage of their choice. It's amazing if you just sit back and watch the magic unfold, only I strongly discourage you to not just sit back and observe because you'll get that label of being "lazy" and not helping to get out of there. Everyone just starts packing up what is nearest to them, whether that was their responsibility for the evening or not. It's like a magnetic force; whatever is nearest clings to you to easily dispose of or put back in its place. When that is finalized, everyone grabs something else, and within approximately twelve minutes, the parking lot is clear and all adult volunteers are manipulating their vehicles home a little over the speed limit, but safely. We are responsible adults after all.

Approximately 180 seconds passed and my nerves leapt due to a subtle vibration emanating from my watch. I keep my phone on silent 24/7. Just makes it easier that it doesn't go off with annoying beeps that I can never find a solution to silence when I'm in classrooms with our amazing students.

Back to the story, my frosty night time beverage is making me wish I would've started the timer on this recipe's "Cook Time." Approximately 180 seconds after I sent my "Thank You" text for helping out at our "Bash," I received a reply from one of the four staff that helped out. This text came from our newest staff member. She wasn't new to the profession, actually had ten years in the game. We were so fortunate that she was willing to come to join our team because she is one of the strongest, most caring, team player teachers I have ever encountered. She replied to my text, which I wasn't expecting to receive anything back from.

"Mike, you're welcome! And this is the first time in all my years an administrator has thanked me for helping at an after-school event. That means a lot!"

I couldn't believe it. Just one little text, to thank the staff for helping out because they knew it was what was needed for our students, and this new teacher to us, who had ten years in the profession, had never gotten a personal, "Thank you."

While nobody ever goes above and beyond solely for the recognition of their superiors or peers, it is a great feeling to be acknowledged for it. The staff that stays after, chaperoning when not asked or required, and sits in the stands to support their students at an athletic event do it because they know it's the right thing to do. **It's all about relationships. Relationships are everything. Relationships are going to build trust, connections, and love that will empower both parties to walk through walls for each other.**

I could have gone about my weekend and not have taken the seven seconds it took to send that text. But I'm glad I did because it served so many more purposes other than letting those staff members know that I appreciated their time the night before. It helped to let that new staff member know that we are in this together, and I acknowledge and am grateful for them going above and beyond their "contract." It helped to build that relationship of trust and respect, something that every administrator and staff member must have to help change the lives of our students for the positive.

I never knew the impact a simple thankful text could have until that Saturday afternoon in September of 2019. I sent more throughout the next few months to show my gratitude, but it wasn't until March of 2020 that I once again experienced the strength of a simple text.

The COVID-19 Pandemic hit us like a sucker punch. By March 17, 2020, our district was solely in remote learning. Students were quarantined at home, as well as all of our staff. We were all in uncharted waters, none of us had ever experienced not only in school and education, but life in this state of our world. Our district had put requirements and protocol in place for staff, but so many staff in our district went above and beyond what was required. Our staff knew that Social-Emotional Learning (SEL) was numero uno during this time, and those Zoom meetings had nothing to do with academics; it was solely people connecting, keeping their relationships and trust strong, and showing concern for each other and their well being.

To be honest, I was struggling during the pandemic. My entire career has been about building relationships, talking face-to-face with others, be it students, families, or staff, and now, being quarantined at home, I was feeling unsuccessful, unaccomplished, and alone. These feelings had me thinking that if I was feeling this way, there was no doubt that some of our staff must be as well. This was new for all of us; none of us knew how to handle the drastic change all of our lives took, especially me. If I was feeling this way, I knew others had to be as well. I have always believed in the power of relationships and relying on our crew, our PLN. The pandemic had me feeling insecure and I needed to help others that may be experiencing the trauma I was going through.

On the evening of Sunday, March 22, 2020, I sent the following text to all of our staff at our school.

"How are you doing?"

That was it. Four words. Every single staff member received their own text, and every single staff member replied within minutes. Some, a simple reply like, "Good, you?" and others wrote sentences and even paragraphs explaining how they were feeling, coping, and what was going on with their families. None of the near sixty conversations discussed school, academics, or curriculum. It was people connecting with and checking on each other. We weren't educators that collaborated at the same school, employed by the same school district. We were friends, family, and human beings caring for one another, and the loved ones we have all shared so many stories about during those "passing periods."

We're all human, and we all need to be noticed, even if we are not expecting or wanting any recognition for it. But when we get acknowledged, it is reassuring we're doing the right thing. During the pandemic, it helped to bring a connection among us, that we were more than just co-workers. I had deeper conversations that evening in March with some staff than I ever had in six years of working alongside one another.

Find time to thank others. Find time to point out that you notice them going above and beyond. In-person is always ideal, but a simple text on a "non-contractual day" is also great. Find ways to let your co-workers know you notice them. Find ways to let our students know you notice them. Find ways to let others know you appreciate them, especially during the trying times. It may mean nothing to you, but to them, it may be just what they needed to get through their day.

TEXTING TOAST

INGREDIENTS

1. One after school hours event
2. Phone numbers of staff members
3. Cell phone
4. Free texting
5. A thankful & grateful attitude

TIME

- Prep Time - One After School Hours Event
- Cook Time - 17 seconds
- Total Time - 1 minute
- Total Cost - Only if your Cell Provider charges per text

PROCEDURE

1. Attend an after school hours event.
2. Take notice of staff that volunteer their time to work/chaperone.
3. The next morning, send a brief text thanking staff that volunteered their time.
4. If more than one staff member volunteered, be sure to text each individually.
5. Brighten someone's day with thoughtful kindness!

A Simple Text
By Melissa Huppert
@HuppertMiss
Kindergarten Teacher

I met Mike the school year before my 12th year of teaching. I considered myself a veteran teacher and had experience working with different types of school leaders. What I had not experienced was someone like Mike. Meeting him for the first time, I could tell he was passionate about his career. But honestly, what educator isn't? Mike brings a contagious positive energy. He is a lead learner who pushes his staff and students to always strive to do their best. He is welcoming, kind, compassionate, and caring. I can remember my first "Back To School Bash" at Oak Glen. I was nervous because I was the new teacher at the school. I worried about making connections. Would it be a good fit? Like any school event, the kids filled my heart. Even better though was the text message I received that evening from Mike. He thanked me for attending the after-school bash and told me he appreciated my commitment to "showing up" for the students. Of all my years in teaching, I had never been told thank you for attending an extracurricular event. In fact, it was just expected. Mike's text message might have taken just a few seconds to send, but it made me feel a part of something great. I knew this school was the right fit, Oak Glen is a great place to work!

10

COMFORT ZONE ZUCCHINI CUPCAKES

"I will never ask you to do anything that I wouldn't do myself."

This was how I opened a staff meeting in January, right after coming back from Winter Break. An extended Winter Break at that. Earlier in the month, our Winter Break was stretched out by four days due to extreme cold weather. When we returned from that Polar Vortex, I held a brief staff meeting, just letting everyone know to not stress about trying to catch up and cram the "learning" in that has been missed. Instead, I said to focus on connections, check-ins, and solidifying the relationships that were already built with students. Many of the staff approached me afterward to let me know how appreciative they were with this mindset as they were feeling anxious about trying to catch up. I just reminded them that it's ALWAYS about relationships, and a longer than scheduled break doesn't change that; it multiplies it! **Without a true relationship, no learning will ever take place.**

At this point, a few weeks after our return, and a few more days off for more extreme cold, we were at our official monthly Staff Meeting. Our Assistant Principal and I were about to take our staff to territories that many administrators are afraid to enter. Let me remind you, this is January, and all of our non-tenured teachers were scheduling their second-round evaluations and many tenured staff were finally getting around to theirs that they had procrastinated about since August.

I stood side-by-side with our Assistant Principal. We had already discussed what we were about to embark on, where we were going to ask the staff to go. We were confident that it would go over smoothly; we had been prepping them by modeling ourselves what we expected for years at this point. Now it was time to give them the push, the nudge over the edge, that many of them needed. Don't hold on, just let go.

"Welcome to a new year. This is the perfect time to set new goals, new initiatives, and try new things. Some of you have ventured out a little bit this year and have tried some new approaches and lessons, but now is the time to really step out of your comfort zone," I confidently said, and let that statement marinate for a few moments.

The room was quiet, none of the staff talked or moved a muscle. All eyes stayed glued on us, waiting for the next piece of information as to what in the world we were talking about. My assistant principal and I were tag-teaming this one, and now it was her turn to shine.

"You guys are an amazing staff, you do a great job reaching all of our students, keeping them engaged and enjoying learning all at the same time. With that being said, we know there's certain approaches or lessons that you may have always wanted to try, but are holding back."

Tag, my turn to launch over the ropes and back into the squared circle.

"That's right. We've been talking about leaving comfort zones all year. Some of you have dabbled outside of your comfort zone a little bit this year, and that is great, but it's time to leave that circle completely. It's time to do what you've always thought about doing in your classroom, something you know the kids would just eat up and be talking about for years! Bring an outside passion of yours into the classroom. It will create a fun and unforgettable day for everyone, but will also allow your students to learn a little about you as a person."

Out of breath, hands resting on my thighs, gasping for air as the sweat pools on the canvas below me. Tag.

"We want all of you to teach a lesson completely out of your comfort zone. This lesson has nothing to do with evaluations, formal or informal. This is just for you, to do and try something that you may have always wanted to try. For you to experiment with a different approach to teaching. For you to have some fun, knowing it is a safe, risk-taking lesson."

I reached out my hand, I needed to get back in.

"That's right, we support you completely. This has nothing, absolutely nothing to do with evaluations. We just want to give you the Green Light to try a lesson, just one, that's all we're asking, out of your comfort zone. We support you and want to help you in any way through this process. Please let us know what you need from us to make this successful. You're good to go, it's ok to try something new, something that may not work out, or may change your approach to teaching for good!"

Time for the last tag, I wanted my comrade to get the final count.

"Again, this has nothing to do with evaluations, but we do want to know when you are completing your Comfort Zone Lesson. We want to know so we can be there so see it, to support you. I'll be sending out a spreadsheet for everyone to put their dates down when you know. You know I love my spreadsheets."

The staff appeared a little hesitant and thrown off like it was a secret "Gotcha" attempt. I'm not sure why they would ever think that. Between both mine and our Assistant Principal's leadership styles, we've never tried to "catch" someone with a negative review or feedback. We've always approached our roles as guides and resources. Administrators are here to help work alongside teachers. We are honest in that we don't have all of the answers or are not experts in everything education-related. We are a team, a family, and the purpose of our role, our title, is to help bring the best education, the best learning experiences, to our students. The only way that is possible is to work side-by-side with one another, not top-down. It doesn't matter if you're a principal, teacher, paraprofessional, bus driver, secretary, or custodian, if you are working in a school you are working to make a difference in kids' lives. We must march together to accomplish this.

It was time for our victory speech. "As I stated at the beginning of the meeting, I would never ask you to do anything that I wouldn't do myself. Take a look at some of the things I have done over the past few years that were out of my comfort zone. I began blogging and sharing it with the world. For my entire life, I have always kept my writing to myself; it's always been used as a personal outlet. I leaped out of my comfort zone and started sharing my blogs, something I now love to do! Kind of cool that if I never left my comfort zone and shared that first blog of mine, you wouldn't be reading this book! Or how about the videos I've been making to share announcements with you and parents? I hate the way I look and sound on video, but the more I make, the more I learn and become more comfortable with it. And podcasting, now that was completely out of my comfort zone! For me to team up with an educator in Arizona, and talk about the connections between punk rock ethos and education, that's insane! But I love it, and wouldn't change it for the world, and it's making a difference for educators."

Our Assistant Principal began to tell stories of how she has gotten out of her comfort zone, especially since joining our family. She told stories of going for runs before the sunrise, something she would never do in years past due to fear of being attacked or hurt. She told an amazing story about seeing Coldplay during a rainstorm. She hates being wet, she hates dancing in public, and she went ahead and did both during the concert. She even went as far as to show a video clip her husband had taken of her, being present and enjoying every moment! Her final story was about how she was new to our district, teaching as a Special Education Resource Teacher at our Middle School. We needed an Assistant Principal as our current one had to leave shortly after the year began. She then met with me and the next thing you know she was going to be our school's new AP! This was a huge adjustment for her in such a short amount of time, but she took on the challenge and is so grateful she did.

She concluded with, "As Mike said, we're never going to ask you to do something that we wouldn't do ourselves."

The first few days were very quiet, like the calm before the storm. Not many, if any, of the staff referenced what was discussed at the faculty meeting. It was almost like, "What happens at the faculty meeting stays at the faculty meeting." Only, we were going to let our secrets out. It was about to get uncomfortable, and that's exactly what we wanted.

About four days passed and I started getting questioned while working at Adina in the halls. I wasn't being questioned on why they needed to leave their comfort zones or ploys to get out of doing it. Instead, all of the questions were asking for approval. I always had the same response, "If you feel that is taking you far out of your comfort zone, do it! **I don't know how much ground your comfort zone covers, only you do. How can I help?"**

This went on for a few days, staff asking for approval, me putting the choice, and power, back in their hands. The following week we finally had some commitments. About half of the staff came directly to me to announce they had decided on what their comfort zone lesson would be and when. I could sense their nervous excitement in them telling me, a sparkle in their eyes, pep in their step, and crackle in their voice. I shared in their enthusiasm, high-fiving, praising the idea, and sometimes even lending a hug. I typically responded with, "This is so awesome, I can't wait! Seriously, let me know what I can do to help, and be sure to add it to the spreadsheet so I can do my best to be there!"

My sharing of excitement and enthusiasm was genuine. I felt just as passionate and stoked for these lessons that would not only take staff out of their comfort zones but also be an event our students would never forget!

I couldn't even fathom the types of lessons that our teachers were bringing to our classrooms and students that were out of their comfort zones. Many of the grade levels chose to do a joint lesson, teaming up with each other to bring an experience like no other to their students. I LOVED this! Our camaraderie was strengthened through collaborating and ensuring that everyone on the team was stepping out of their comfort zone. It built chains of trust. These teams knew that they had each other's backs and that no matter how strenuous, difficult, or uncomfortable a situation one may be faced with, their teammates, their crew, would be there to help push them through it. And when their peer was facing something, they would be there for them.

There wasn't one Comfort Zone Lesson that I was disappointed with, nor could I pick a favorite. Some lessons were something simple, like recording a video of themselves to explain a concept and have the students watch it. While for some this doesn't seem like much, for others it is a huge leap out of their comfort zone circle. That is exactly what this exercise was about; individuals stepping out of THEIR comfort zones. Not mine, not yours, not their neighbors, but THEIRS.

The Comfort Zones Lessons were amazing! We had a teacher, who was in the choir during high school and college, record himself singing a lesson to his students...on a video recording! Double points!

Another, who is an amazing facilitator with group discussions, had her students enter an Escape Room! Her classroom door was locked, lights off, and curtains were drawn, and class began in the hallway. The teacher explained to the students they were about to enter an escape room, where they needed to find the secret antidote to survive. Once inside, students got into their groups, which they already knew, and watched instructions from the doctor on how they would work together to find the antidote. Once they got the "Go!", teams were opening their envelopes, problem-solving, and collaborating on various math concepts and standards before moving onto the next clue. While there was a clear "winner" on which group finished first, it was so pleasing to see each group cheering on the next, providing praise and motivation until every group found their antidote, even after the time limit expired.

The fourth-grade team chose to work together, turning their entire section of the hallway into an ER wing. Students came into class in the morning to find surgical coats, masks (yep, this was before we HAD to wear masks around each other), and gloves. Students, I'm sorry, the young Residents, were told by their instructing Doctors that after they returned from their Specials class, they would be conducting open-heart surgery. After the 35-minute Special, the Residents entered the operating room, giddy and excited. They took their spots at their operating tables, waiting for instructions. Next to each surgical bed was a file for their patient, including documents and forms they would need to fill out pre-, during, and post-surgery. For the actual procedure, the Residents needed to extract a piece of paper, think of a small scroll, from the inside of a Jell-O mold heart. They were to use tweezers and steel kabob sticks, doing their very best to keep the heart intact. After the scroll was extracted, students had a series of mathematical problems to complete based on the heartbeat that was listed on the scroll. After all of the surgeries were finished, the Residents went through a series of exercises like jumping jacks and burpees, led by the main Doctors, to then measure, compare, and contrast their own heartbeats and pulse rates before and after breaking a sweat.

First grade needed a little help from me to pull off their Comfort Zone Lesson. Every year they have a unit that revolves around Fairy Tales and concludes with the story of Cinderella. Two days before the first grade was concluding their Fairy Tale unit, I rode into each of the classrooms on my noble steed, carrying a basket of important scrolls. Of course my noble steed was my trusty skateboard.

"Hear ye, hear ye! I am here to formally invite you all to Cinderella's Crystal Ball just two days from today! There will be dancing, treats, and fun for all! Please dress in your best as the Princess herself will be in attendance!"

Anticipation was built in the days leading up to the Crystal Ball. The teachers didn't avoid the topic but instead embraced it. They let the students know how excited they were to be a part of Cinderella's Crystal Ball. They facilitated discussions on what is found at a formal event. Unanimously, the students in all four of our first-grade classes knew, dancing! The teachers spent time in the afternoon teaching students how to formally Waltz so everyone could enjoy time on the dance floor at the Crystal Ball.

The day had finally arrived. Students came dressed to impress! Their outfits were better than those worn on picture day! Hair was done, jewelry was donned, and nothing but chivalry could be found in the first-grade wing. The Crystal Ball officially started after lunch. Students lined up against their lockers. Even the kindergarten and second-grade classes filled the halls remaining in the wing to catch a glimpse of the Princess. The horns sounded and out of Room 101 floated Princess Cinderella herself! She was accompanied by her three maidens. The Princess thanked everyone for attending her ball. After her speech, the music began and all of the attendees began waltzing! Princess Cinderella couldn't find her Prince Charming, but instead chose a peasant in blue jeans, a t-shirt, hoody, and skateboard to share a dance with!

The Comfort Zone Lessons were so much more than just forcing staff to do something they have never done before. Every individual came out of their comfort zone lesson smiling, laughing, and feeling accomplished for successfully stepping out of their circle and conquering a challenge. Whenever we step outside our comfort zones, we grow a little bit more. Our staff now was much more confident bringing lessons similar to the one they just completed to their classroom.

Our staff also learned the power of collaboration and relying on your crew. As I mentioned earlier, many of the staff worked as a team to plan and implement their lessons. This lent itself to relying upon and trusting their teammates, especially during situations where one is not an expert and journeying into uncharted territory. They learned about each other's strengths and gained confidence in admitting their areas of growth to their team. Schoolwide, staff were asking one another what their lessons were, how they came about it and then encouraged one another to successfully execute theirs! Everyone was supportive of each other and shared in the excitement!

Some of the best outcomes were what I thought could only be cooked up in dreams. If you remember from the Tag Team Wrestling Speech I presented with our Assistant Principal, we kept emphasizing that these lessons had nothing, I repeat NOTHING, to do with evaluations. Not formal or informal. Yet, many, about 80% of the staff that was up for a formal evaluation, chose this to be their observation! YES, they were that confident that a lesson, out of their comfort zone, something they were taking a risk on, was to be their formal observation for the school year. This speaks volumes! Our staff was confident in themselves, their colleagues and teammates, and me and our AP that they wouldn't fail. They trusted us, the administrators, that the Comfort Zone Lesson was supported and we meant what we said. Education is about taking risks, walking out on a limb, to continually improve ourselves to be better for kids. We ask our students to take risks every day, so why should educators be any different?

Finally, all of the lessons were not only fun, engaging, and risk-taking for the educators, they also had the same effect on our students. Every student loved the fresh approach their teacher brought to their class.

Students were going to remember the experiences that their teachers shared with them for years to come. The best part was that all of these lessons, with the costumes, theatrics, gimmicks, voice changes, songs, and props were some of the most in-depth, cross-curricular, and deep learning lessons I have ever seen. With some fun, creativity, and risk-taking, there are no boundaries to true, life-changing learning.

COMFORT ZONE ZUCHINI CUPCAKES

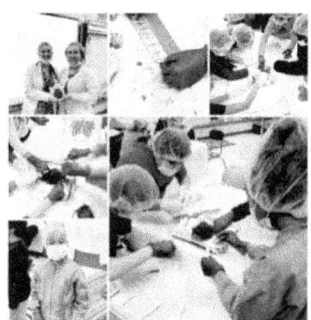

INGREDIENTS

1. Personally know your comfort zone
2. Have dreams of what one has always wanted to do in the classroom but has held back
3. Supervisors modeling leaving their comfort zones
4. Trust
5. Relationships
6. Creativity

TIME

- Prep Time - 14 days
- Cook Time - 60 minutes
- Total Time - 2 weeks 1 hour
- Total Cost - Various

PROCEDURE

1. First & foremost, a trusting relationship must be in place between all parties.
2. Supervisors, whether it's admin to teacher or teacher to student, must model and share ways they leave their comfort zones. Best if this is done weeks & months in advance, not just a one-time thing.
3. Supervisors share how they leave their comfort zones & the impact it's made on them.
4. Brainstorm together, ideas, approaches, & lessons one has always wanted to do, but has held back on.
5. Examine why this has never been put into practice.
6. Create a plan for the lesson or activity that will take you out of your comfort zone.
7. Set the date the comfort zone lesson will happen.
8. Gather all materials, if any.
9. Play out the lesson by yourself, in your head, in front of your dog, or anyone, to get a feel for doing something you're not familiar with.
10. About 3 days before the lesson, hype up the staff, or kids, about what they will embark on. Share YOUR enthusiasm.
11. Play out the lesson, having fun with it, being flexible if things don't go as planned, & share laughs & memories.
12. Reflect.
13. Plan your next exit from your now larger comfort zone!

Comfort Zones
By Spencer White
@Spencer94665541
Special Education Teacher

Comfort zones are very easy to get stuck into. We get busy and we just do the same thing repeatedly. People are also very hesitant to get out of their comfort zones because we, as human beings, do not usually like to feel uncomfortable. However, we as teachers can benefit from teaching outside our comfort zones, mainly to the benefits of the students.

Teaching special education can be a challenge to do a lesson outside a comfort zone. The reason for this is students with special needs have a hard time handling lessons that are more spontaneous and unstructured. So, when planning a lesson like this, keep in mind these two things. Make sure to keep some form of structure and give your students a heads up about the lesson. Doing these two things will help with these types of lessons.

Now, let us get to my example of a Comfort Zone lesson. We were sitting in a faculty meeting and then my administrative team came up with the idea of getting us to teach a lesson outside of our comfort zones. When I heard this, I was a little nervous to do this because of the reasons stated above about my population of students. So, I thought about what I could even do to get out of my comfort zone. Then it came to me. I like to sing, but I would never really do it in front of my students. This is how I decided to do a lesson outside of my comfort zone by having students show their talents.

This was a great opportunity to use a feature in one of my educational tools I use in my classroom. I used a feature to record myself explaining the lesson, and I wanted the students to record themselves demonstrating a talent that they have, it could be dancing or even singing. After I explained the directions through the video, I then showed them my talent of singing and sang them a song. My students were so engaged throughout this whole video.

Once the video was done, you could feel the excitement that my students had to start this lesson. I told them they could spread out across the classroom and practice what they wanted to show me through their video. When they were ready to record their video, they were able to go into a corner of the room that I had blocked off, so no one could see them. This allowed them to feel comfortable showing me their talent in the video.

The videos were amazing. I was so proud of them to be willing to show me a side of themselves that they might have not been comfortable to show. I think one thing that helped them was me showing some vulnerability in singing on the video and showing it to them.

Getting out of our comfort zones can be a challenge. We can simply say I like my comfy spot I am in. However, we need to think about how amazing it can be for our students. This can be a great teachable moment in showing them the value that it is fine to feel uncomfortable sometimes. Allowing students to see the benefit of taking risks and jumping into something new that they may have never tried before doesn't have to be a scary event. Just remember comfort zones are easy to get stuck in, but do not be afraid to jump out of them to enhance your students' educational experiences.

11

SELFLESS SLIDERS

I will never forget the palpable air that filled the room during one of my first speaking gigs at a national educational conference. I had told my story of being a classroom teacher, like many of those in the audience, that beat to his own punk rock double bass drum. This quickly turned to me conforming to the stereotypes and expectations of educational administration when I took my first Principalship. After two quick and swift years, I almost left the profession. I did a lot of deep soul searching, discovered and connected with some amazing educators throughout the country, and took the Principalship in a direction that many had never seen...my way. I then shared many of the relationship-building techniques that you've read in our previous recipes already. Everything was going great, there was laughter, smiles, applause, and then I declared the following words.

"You need to put yourself before others. Yes, we're educators; students and staff depend on us. Yes, we have families; they need us. But I want you to think of yourself, and more importantly, PUT yourself first."

All of the good vibes that I had built up, the positivity of the future of our classrooms and schools for those educators sharing the room with me, was gone as fast as the Bee Gees disappearing once the Ramones emerged. The end of Poison with Nirvana. A million thoughts slam danced in my mind, but I knew I could bring this audience back. I hadn't fully lost the lifeline. I've only shared an ⅛ of this last message.

All eyes were on me, some jaws on the floor, and the owners of those that weren't had their heads tilted, as if pointing an ear towards my direction would somehow bring about the answer they couldn't find on their own.

"Yes, you heard me right, you must put yourself before others. Honestly, those close to you may say it's selfish, and they're right, but only if you make it a selfish act."

I've been in education for nearly twenty years. Some years I have been extremely effective in making a difference in kids' lives, others not so much. Hell, even now I'm effective some weeks and the next not at all. As I've gotten older, I've been engaging in a lot of self-reflection. Those times when I could have done more and been there more for others are the times when I wasn't taking care of myself first.

I truly believe that to be the most world-changing and inspiring educator, to be the spouse and parent that our families need and deserve, we must first take care of ourselves.

If we aren't putting our health, wellness, and mindfulness first, how can we do that for others? If we are not in the right mental and emotional state of mind, how can we lead others to their own?

To be an effective influencer, guide, and world-changer, we must take care of ourselves. This looks different for every individual. For some, it may be training and eventually running anything from a 5K to a full 26.2 mile marathon. Some choose to challenge the iron because according to Henry Rollins, the iron never lies. 200 pounds is always

200 pounds (2012). Breaking a sweat, regardless of the means, is one avenue many travel when searching for self-care.

Not everyone can release endorphins via exercise, and that is completely fine. Maybe gardening brings you to your zen state. Reading for pleasure, writing, and journaling have also been known to do the trick. Spending each morning in a mindful state, whether that be in prayer, meditation, or enjoying a cup of coffee while gazing out of your back window and taking in the beauty of the world around us during those solitude moments can all lead one to self-care.

The beauty of self-care is that whatever brings YOU peace, whatever clears YOUR mind, whatever calms YOU is self-care.

"Putting ourselves first is only selfish if we do it at the expense of others."

Jaws were picked up off of the floor, heads were no longer trying to impersonate an owl, and the natural act of breathing returned to my audience.

"So let me explain what I mean by practicing self-care not at the expense of others. What are your spouse and family going to say if you've been gone all day, giving your all for students and staff, walk in your front door and you say, 'All Right, I'm going to the gym for an hour.'"

There were some head nods, a few mumbles. I did the ten-second pause and wait we expect to see in our classrooms when a question is posed.

"Look, I have a wife of 12 years and two beautiful kids, 11 and 8. They're great, a handful, but awesome. I must be there for them. I can't expect my wife to do it all. That's not a partnership."

A brave soul in the crowd raised their hand, high above the crowns of their peers. "How do you do it then? How do you find time to train and run marathons, read, and write? Those are your three self-care practices, right?"

"Great question! And we're going to get to that. First, I need to explain why we need to take care of ourselves."

I've discovered that when I am not putting myself first, when I'm not working out in the morning regularly at least 5 days per week, when I'm not watching my diet and what is being ingested into my body, and when I don't read or write for at least 30 minutes each night, I am not in a positive state. I am not mentally, physically, emotionally, or even spiritually sound.

When those busy weeks hit like a solid brick wall and the enemy mind claims sleep is more important than an early morning run. When the donut, pizza, and french fries taste more satisfying due to stress than the spinach smoothie sitting in the fridge. When I'd rather sit on the couch with an ice-cold IPA, vegging out mindlessly watching reality television after a busy, stressful day as opposed to writing with a glass of ice water or hot tea next to me. When one of these scenarios plays out, there is a 99% chance that the others will follow within the next day, playing out like Bill Murray in Groundhog Day. Once that hits, I feel like garbage that needs to be thrown out and disposed of. Pretty much useless.

When I enter that state, and I won't lie, it still happens after understanding the importance of self-care, I am not effective for my staff or students. The energy is gone. The motivation is gone. The drive to help others, to listen to their problems, and help them get out of their hole, is gone. I go through the school day like a trained robot, flowing through the motions. Sometimes I will get back on track by lunchtime, and turn it around, but those morning minutes are gone. And that is not fair to our staff, and most importantly, our students. We can never make up for time wasted and lost.

Homelife is no different. I've discovered that when I do not practice self-care regularly, when those lazy, couch potato symptoms mentioned in the above paragraph take control, I have less energy and focus than when I am waking early before the majority of the country. This, not taking time for my own self-care, adds stress to my wife, who now has to pick up the slack that I'm leaving for her. My kids see me as someone they can not turn to for help, support, attention, and love. This is something that I promised myself would never happen long before we welcomed my first son into this world.

"When do I find the time to take care of myself when I have a wonderful wife, two amazing, active kids, and leading a school of 65 amazing educators and 525 future world-changers? That's easy, when they're asleep."

I've learned that as my kids have gotten older their activities, homework, and staying up later have put a damper on my evening workouts. With them having more needs, my responsibility as their dad is to be there for them, to help them through their evening activities, to support my wife and work as a team. By the time they do get to bed, the sun has been hidden for hours and my fuel tank gauge is nearing "E."

It has taken many hypotheses and experiments to find what is the best approach for me to still get in my self-care to make me the servant leader and team player my staff, stakeholders, and most importantly, students deserve, and also the most supportive, loving, and all-in husband and dad my family deserves.

For me, my alarm goes off at 4:05 a.m. three days per week, Monday, Wednesday, and Thursday. Tuesday and Friday are for my wife to get in her self-care in the early hours. Saturday and Sunday I get to sleep in. The weekends I'm up and out the door by 6:00 a.m. Sometimes it's earlier depending on if it's marathon training season and a long run is on the schedule. That wasn't a typo. Waking at 6:00 a.m. on the weekends IS sleeping in.

Many cringe, and sigh when I share my self-care time. That's fine, it's not for everyone. It's for me. This is what works best for me in my life right now. Five years down the road it may change, but I can guarantee that I will always find a schedule to take care of myself. I must if I am going to be the leader our staff, students, and families deserve. I must if I am going to be the husband my wife deserves and the dad my kids need.

Find what self-care activities help to clear your mind, to bring you inspiration and motivation, to better serve others and be there for them. Once you know that activity, find the time to practice it. Some may need to only do it once a day per week, while others, like myself, need to practice self-care at least five days a week. Once you find that balance, and like every scale will adjust with time, find when you can do this without sacrificing moments with others. If the activity is at the expense of time you have to serve them then self-care is just selfishness.

To help inspire others to be confident in themselves and become determined to change the world begins with ourselves. We must take care of ourselves first, families and loved ones second, and our school families third. If we try to do this in any other order, we will not successfully make a difference in any.

SELFLESS SLIDERS

INGREDIENTS

1. Have a passion, hobby, or activity that you enjoy doing for YOU
2. A total of 35 minutes
3. Alarm Clock
4. Discipline to awake 30 minutes earlier each day

TIME

- Prep Time - 5 minutes
- Cook Time - 30 minutes
- Total Time - 35 minutes
- Total Cost - $0.00

PROCEDURE

1. Understand that your self-care is a necessity to be a benefit to others in your life.
2. Declare to yourself that you will not allow the busyness of life to take you away from your self-care passions.
3. Declare to yourself & loved ones that your self-care passion will not take away time from them.
4. Set your alarm clock for at least 30 minutes earlier than you typically wake up.
5. Know that discipline > motivation. Get up when the alarm goes off & complete your self-care activity.
6. If mornings aren't your thing, you can always complete your self-care passion in the late evening hours after all of your loved ones are settled. (But there is a satisfaction of getting it done first thing in the morning!)

Fill Your Cup So You Can Pour Onto Others
By Santiago Meza
@santiagoAM115
Principal

Family is not just important but it is essential in one's life. The people who are in your family by blood, those that you have met along the way in life, your staff, your community, your students, they are all part of your family. All these different families meld into one going through your days. It's hard work being in families. They require time, effort, and love to make the bonds stay strong and grow. Families also require emotional support and guidance consistently and constantly if we are going to make family relationships work. The time that you spend with your family is priceless. You go all out all the time for the ones you love.

It's hard to juggle your school family time and your own family time at home and not cross the two where your time is sacrificed to by either or both. They both play an important role in your life and both need your undivided attention. All this time spent with your families can take all your energy and time, but you can't give all the time and energy to them if you are running on empty. You need to care for yourself to care for others.

Some people would call it selfish for wanting to care for yourself. You are not being selfish for wanting to care for yourself; you are being selfless in trying to regain strength, endurance, and stamina to carry the families that you love in and out of school.

You don't have to sacrifice family and self-care; you just have to find a balance that replenishes you so you can care for families. Only by taking care of yourself can you truthfully and wholeheartedly care for others that depend on you and need you for support.

Spend no less than 30 minutes a day for YOU time. This is time spent when you should be doing something for yourself that revives the soul and gets your mind right. Self-care is as important as the time you spent on others. The time spent on self to build a strong self-care foundation will lead to stronger ways to love and support your families to keep your relationships strong and thriving.

12

FLIPPIN' FLAPJACKS

February, uuuggghhh...the shortest month of the year, yet for educators, it is one of the most dreaded. You wake up and it's dark outside. Shower, throw on your "work" clothes and they're feeling just a little bit more snug from the holiday indulgences the past two months. You spend eight hours motivating, inspiring, and pulling everything out of your toolbox only to fight against the "Holiday Hangover" our students are now experiencing. Motivation is down, enthusiasm is one flicker away from burning out, and then you remember next month begins state testing. What a perfect time for our great states to judge our students, and your effectiveness as a classroom teacher or leader of a school, over a few days when we have just been trying to get through the month. You leave school, exhausted. It's dark outside.

I'm not sure about your school and district, but in mine, February is the busiest month, especially for elementary school administrators. Round Two of Teacher Evaluations has begun. We also have our Science Fairs. Yes, you read that correctly; Fairs is plural. We have our Elementary Science Fair, bringing together our three elementary buildings. This is held on a Saturday. Young scientists that are ranked "Outstanding" by our community judges are invited to compete in our District's Area Science Fair. The Elementary Scientists that were invited, as well as every

Middle School Scientist that was ranked "Outstanding" in their fair are who comprise the Area Science Fair. This Middle School Science Fair I just spoke of is held on a Saturday. Granted it's the last Saturday of January, but c'mon, after the holidays everything meshes together like a freshly packed snowball. Oh, and I forgot to mention, that Area Fair is invite-only? Yep, Saturday.

Usually, at this point in my stories, we do a Tarantino break to a real life scenario to help cook up some tasty treats to keep you coming for more. This chapter we're not. This chapter will drag on a little bit longer than we all anticipated, just like February. A long, slow, simmer.

February. Let's see. We've covered the Science Fairs. Did I mention the Elementary Basketball Season? Tryouts begin before Winter Break in December. Much of the season takes place in January, but it does roll into February. Then there is the annual Roundball Classic. This is a three-day tournament between our District's three elementary teams as well as the private school teams in our town. The tournament begins on a Thursday evening, Day Two is Friday evening, and finally, the tournament rounds conclude throughout Saturday morning and afternoon. Everyone takes a rest on Sunday before the Awards Ceremony and Championship Game on Monday evening! That's an abundance of elementary school basketball in a short amount of time.

Now please don't take the opening of this chapter as me complaining and having a negative viewpoint as to participating and being present at all of the extracurricular functions during February. I love attending all of these events! Not one is "required" per se, but I still attend them all, even if I am not in charge of running the event. It is important for not only our students and families to know I support and believe in them and want to share in their growth and success outside of the classroom, but it is also important for me to be there. My job as a school principal is not about raising test scores and managing a school from crumbling. My responsibility as a school principal is to influence lives to make a positive change in our world. That is only going to happen by first having a strong, trusting, relationship. By attending these after-hour events, it shows to our students and families that they are believed in and supported.

Flippin' Flapjacks

"Hey, what's wrong? You all right?" my Assistant Principal asked as I sat at her desk, inhaling a big sigh of air, and meshing my forehead to my palms.

Without breaking the mold of my newly sculptured posture, I replied, "No, I'm fine, I'm just exhausted. I'm so damn tired."

She responded with, "Yeah, me too, February is hard, I can tell everyone is feeling it."

I didn't say a word, I just slowly tilted my head to the right 90 degrees to peer out her office window. Our Assistant Principal's office is located in the middle of the school, right at the busy intersection of 4th, 5th, and RTI hallways. What I saw out that window verified what our assistant principal stated.

Teachers, walking their students to Specials classes and bathroom breaks. Heads down, silent mouths, feet shuffling in unison. It resembled an organized zombie outbreak. Our staff and students were not moving as the undead because they were bored or depressed, they were exhausted. The hard work of expanding minds, the holidays, and extracurriculars had finally caught up and was draining the excitement and fun we all long for during our learning.

I needed to do something, I needed to stop this outbreak before it became too overrun and strong to be taken down. I needed something everyone loved. I needed pancakes.

My daughter's angelic voice pirouetted throughout our kitchen, "Dad, they look like they're starting to bubble. Is it time to flip them?"

I turned on my teacher's voice so she could hear my warning over the blaring volume of my son's video games from across the room. "Hold on babe, I'm coming, don't do anything, I don't want you to get burned."

I skipped back to not only ensure she was staying safe (which of course she was) and to make sure we weren't eating pancakes resembling hockey pucks in color.

"Alright, so you were correct. When they start to bubble like that we need to flip them over so they don't burn. I'll show you how and then you can try it on your own with me here. You need to be careful; that pan is hot!"

I then slowly and carefully flipped over a half-cooked pancake to demonstrate.

"Now you try," I said in a tone of confidence and belief in her as I handed her the spatula.

Her first attempt was kind of a mess. Half of the pancake landed right on the edge of the pan while the other half was outside of the pan, basically forming a strong bond with the stovetop. She looked disappointed.

"Don't worry, you got this. You don't have to flip it as I did. I've been doing this for a while. Find what works for you. We've got more than enough batter and I promise we'll have enough to eat."

I then watched her not pick up another pancake as high, but carefully use the edge of the pan as leverage to flip it over and land directly on its uncooked side in our pan.

Success and smiles!

Flippin' Flapjacks

Faculty meetings are mandatory in our district. I've talked to other principals that tell me if they don't have anything to report on, or it can be done via email, Google Classroom, or Zoom, they don't have one. Our teacher's contract states that they must attend a one-hour faculty meeting every month. By now you hopefully realize that our faculty meetings are enjoyable and staff looks forward to...except for February.

Our meeting was scheduled for Wednesday. This conversation you're about to become a part of took place on Tuesday, the day before.

"Mike, are we really having a meeting tomorrow? Can't we just go home? I feel like we just had one. I look forward to what you have us do, but c'mon, I know you're exhausted too."

I had those sentences spoken to me by many staff members this Tuesday. I always gave the same reply, with fake enthusiasm, "Don't worry, it's going to be awesome as they always are. You'll enjoy it!"

Fake it 'till you make it, right? Also, here's a little secret. I had no idea, literally, nothing planned that was going to make tomorrow's meeting "awesome!"

Tuesday night came, I zoned out on the couch, completely numbing my brain with mindless television. I dropped the ball and did not plan anything for my promised "awesome" faculty meeting in less than 24 hours.

Wednesday morning had my watch alarm vibrating to get me out of bed at 4:05 am. I knew that I needed a miracle to save this meeting coming up and the only way to get the creative juices flowing again was a good gym session.

As I was completing some supplemental lifts after a heavy deadlift session, I began to think of how hungry I was. My mind wandered to that Saturday morning a few years back when I taught my daughter how to flip pancakes. I wished I had enough time to make pancakes before work. Today those wouldn't be happening...or would they?

Our February staff meeting was about to begin. I had a genuine smile that grew from ear to ear. No more faking it. I couldn't wait to get this meeting going! I had some damage control. Typically, I feed our staff some appetizers, little teasers, leading up to the meeting. This month all I had given them was a generic, off-brand, government-issued "awesome."

"All right, we're going to get started. I have a few items to run through, but then we are going to head over to the gym for the main dish of our meeting."

Heads perked up; comrades made curious eye gazes at one another. I had them; they were getting wafts of that beautiful scent drifting out from the kitchen. They knew this would be an awesome staff meeting, just as ours always were. Even in cold, dark, February.

We got through the standard materials that needed to be covered and discussed. Then it was time to give a little breakdown, some instructions on what was to come, much like a chef preparing guests for the next plate during a five-course meal.

"Ok. Before we head over to the gym, I need you to grab partners and form a team. Each team needs to have at least one teacher from each grade level, as well as a specialist and paraprofessional. I've had a lot of coffee today, so I'm going to run to the restroom. See everyone in the gym in 180 seconds. When you get in there, stand with your team so I can easily spot who is working with who."

And then I made a mad dash to relieve my bladder.

Upon entering the gym, I saw about seven teams set up. They followed directions and had the perfect variety and mix in each one. Also, in the corner, was our butcher paper roll which I had wheeled in about 45 minutes prior.

I stood on the stage, high above the teams who were about to compete against one another.

"First, declare a captain. You have fifteen seconds."

Within about seven seconds, all captains were named and stepped forward.

"Now, each captain needs to go and rip off a piece of butcher paper. It doesn't matter which color, just not black. The paper needs to be long enough for every member of your team to stand on it. Once you have your paper, lay it on the ground, make a mark, symbol, or write your team name on the top side, and have everyone stand on it."

An outsider would've thought that this was a back-to-school activity with the excitement, smiles, and laughter that permeated the gym air.

"I wanted pancakes today, so this afternoon, we're 'Flippin' Flapjacks!' How it works, each team needs to flip their flapjack, their paper, completely over without ripping it or having anyone stepping or touching the gym floor."

There was a shout mixed with fear and frustration from the arena. "But none of us have the same sized paper? That's not fair."

I had thought of this earlier but didn't have time myself to get all even pieces for everyone. Luckily, I was firing on all cylinders today from that early morning deadlift session.

"I left it up to the captains to get a piece big enough for all to stand on. That's on your captain. When you cook pancakes is each one always the same shape? Nope. All right, here we go. The first three teams to flip their flapjack win a prize! GO!!!"

Each team had a different strategy, a different approach. Every cook has their own pizzazz when preparing a dish.

Some teams got close together; then each lifted one foot for a little fold of the paper. In unison, all of their feet returned to the paper. Next, the other foot. It resembled a well-oiled machine.

Another team crowded as close as they could to one another at one end of the paper. One member then pulled the opposite end towards them. Everyone carefully walked onto the now flipped side. Then, the same approach to finish the flip.

My favorite strategy, but not the most successful or graceful, had some members on the backs of their peers, looking like they were ready for a Chicken Fight rather than Flippin' Flapjacks. I had to look away quickly because I'm pretty sure this approach isn't approved in our annual mandated safety training.

Among all of the teams, not one approach was the same. The only similarities each team shared were communication, collaboration, support of one another, and laughter. There was a lot of laughter for a February Faculty Meeting.

After we had our first three teams finished, we didn't call the challenge. We kept it going, and now everyone who was already finished was supporting, encouraging, and helping those still working. It wasn't a competition of who was the best, but we all, regardless of the team we chose to be on, needed to complete this challenge. It didn't matter if your team was first, fourth, or last. When everyone successfully flipped their flapjack, we all won!

"All right, we have our top three teams! Congratulations to everyone. It was great to see the different approaches all of you took. Even though everyone was different in their plan of attack, each path led to success. Some faster than others and those of you who finished in the tail end needed more support from those already done, but isn't that exactly like our classrooms? Don't we have students, at every level, needing varying degrees of support? Didn't it make a difference the more and more your peers chimed in to help as they finished? **Now imagine a classroom, where everyone, literally EVERYONE, is supportive of each other regardless of their differences or where they are on their learning path. Imagine how far EVERYONE will go that year?"**

I let that little motivational nugget sink in for thirty seconds before continuing.

"Now, let's get to the prizes!"

If you ask me, every prize I give out is always amazing! Our staff may have a much different opinion. Regardless, every challenge they still work hard to earn whatever is. Because each prize is of the Heavens, I couldn't pick one to be the best for first place and down. Instead, I called upon the captains to make this decision.

"This team finished first. Before you can claim your prize, please explain your approach and why you feel this led to your victory?"

The captain explained their team's methodical approach. As they spoke, their colleagues and opponents nodded in amazement as not thinking of such a simple way to lead to success.

"Since you are the victors, and your tactics were near flawless, you get to pick your prize. I have three different prizes in this box." I held up a small cardboard box and shook it high above my head.

"There's Green, Yellow, and Red, like the stoplight. What color prize do you choose?"

The captain turned to their teammates, looking for what they all agreed would be the best choice. Again, each prize was a winner…in my eyes.

"Green. We take Green," was what the captain muttered hesitantly.

"You don't seem confident, but you all get a bookmark with our school logo on it!" I shouted with the excitement of someone winning the grand prize on a cheesy game show.

Much of the same happened when the second-place team was asked to claim their prize. They chose Yellow, which was a yellow band representing my podcast, Punk Rock Classrooms. Check us out at www.punkrockclassrooms.com!

Third place, they just got what was left, which was a Jeans Day Pass. Now, many argue that the Jeans Day Pass is the best prize, but c'mon, who doesn't want a bookmark with their school's mascot or a pencil yellow band sporting their boss's podcast?

Flippin' Flapjacks is a recipe that is so much more than bringing joy to a staff that is feeling the drudgery of mid-year stress, holiday hangovers, and a Chicagoland winter. Flippin' Flapjacks is about communication, collaboration, listening, and getting out of our comfort zones and getting close to one another. From our day in the kitchen together cooking pancakes, it was clear that we all need each other's support. My only suggestion is if you cook up this dish with your students or staff, measure out the pieces to be equal...or not, those brief moments of disbelief and feeling of not being on a level playing field are priceless!

FLIPPIN' FLAPJACKS

INGREDIENTS
1. Butcher paper
2. Large, open area (gym)
3. Pen
4. Teamwork
5. Trust
6. Communication

TIME
- Prep Time - 5 minutes
- Cook Time - 30 minutes
- Total Time - 35 minutes
- Total Cost - $11.97

PROCEDURE
1. Have individuals break into groups of 5-8 members.
2. Each group should have a representative from different areas, i.e., different grade levels.
3. Each group chooses or nominates a captain.
4. Each captain gets a piece of butcher paper large enough for every member to stand on at the same time.
5. Each group is to mark the top & bottom of their butcher paper.
6. Groups will either have a set amount of time or until everyone completes the activity of flipping the paper over.
7. All members stand on top of the butcher paper & begin the timer.
8. Without stepping off of the butcher paper or onto the floor groups must completely flip the butcher paper over.
    a. To accomplish this groups will utilize:
        i. Communication
        ii. Collaboration
        iii. Trust
        iv. Teamwork
9. After each group has completed, or time is up, debrief & have each group share their approach & discuss its effectiveness.
    a. What worked well?
    b. What could be improved?
10. If prizes are being given, distribute after each group has shared their approach.

Getting Close
By Bridgett Annicks
Teacher

Often teachers dread faculty meetings and professional development days. Teachers are known to not make the best students. Therefore, to keep teachers engaged as we would our students, it is imperative to have hands-on, cooperative, thought-provoking activities for these meetings.

One afternoon, we were called to the gym and told to form groups of 10 people. Next, we had to stand in two rows, shoulder to shoulder. Then we pulled roll paper about two feet longer than our group. We were to draw an X on it and then stand on it. The objective was to flip our paper over without getting off of it.

To say we got very close to each other quickly, would be an understatement. Each person had a different idea as to how to do it. It was evident in the groups the people who were quick to take charge and those who followed directions.

This activity tested our problem-solving, communication, and teamwork skills. Unfortunately, our group was not successful, but quite a few other groups completed the task.

Hint: Try to fold the paper over to the side like an L shape instead of directly pulling it over.

Forming Relationships
By Cheryl Barbaro
Teacher

Every day, people are faced with a choice, the choice to do the same thing that they do every day, or the choice to exert the energy to go beyond. I often find that in the classroom, this choice is very apparent and crucial at the beginning of a school year. I find myself investing in the students that most would not find the time for. Many students are just trying to survive; be the educator that they cannot ignore and the one that changes their life. One positive affirmation can stick with a student and make an impact on their future.

As educators, we often do not see how our students are affected by us after they leave our classrooms. I try to form relationships and build their self-esteem hoping it will carry them far beyond the walls of my classroom. I have worked with students outside of a school setting and feel that positivity is what is lacking in most students' lives. Why not be the person that makes another person feel empowered? I want to be the person that empowers a child and allows them to see that the sky is the limit, a person that reminds others everyone deserves a chance to be the best version of themselves. As an educator, I have the power to influence a child and change the direction they thought their life was going. Every child deserves to be celebrated and reach their true potential! Every student deserves to thrive in every element of life.

13

POP PUNK PASSION PIZZA

Punk Rock is more than just a phase I experienced as a confused and lost teen. It was an escape from the stresses, anxiety, and hardships adolescents go through. This included school, home life, and other scenarios we create in our own young and growing minds. I often felt like an outcast, left alone on an island as no one else understood what I was experiencing or going through. There was always one place I could turn to escape the shakes, tears, screams, and angst that had festered inside of my confused body. Punk Rock.

Before any of my crew had a driver's license, it was CDs. I have always had an addictive personality, and each week I got my fix on Tuesday. Every Tuesday I made my way, usually a ride from my mom, to the local independent record stores. I'd save my lawn mowing and chore money to purchase new music each week. If I had a bad day at school, if I was angry with my parents, if I had relationship issues, or if I just needed to escape it all, my CDs transported me to another place. With my outside noise-canceling headphones on, I'd study the lyrics, listening, reading, and escaping from any of the chains that had been holding me down. Music was, scratch that, still is my drug and wipes away the fog on my mirror so I can see myself clearly.

Once the crew hit 16, it was a new chapter. Now we were able to spend nearly every Friday and Saturday night at a local coffee house, bowling alley, or Standing Room Only venue in the big city of Chicago! It wasn't until I was able to experience punk rock and hardcore shows live that I truly broke through that locked bathroom door, no longer needing that mirror to see. Being amongst others like me, dancing, moshing, skanking (yes, I LOVED the ska music revival and STILL listen to ska all of the time), and singing along to the songs we so connected with was the relief I needed. If CDs were a gateway, live shows are the heavy stuff.

Punk Rock teaches youth so many strong character qualities that will carry them through life. Unity, there's a sense of camaraderie amongst those in the scene. We look out for each other and want nothing more than to see the success of one another. We are there for each other, lending a basement couch to sleep on, or loaning a few bucks to help someone who may be our BFF or just a mere acquaintance so they can get a taco or two and some cinnamon twists to eat. Punk Rock brings us together, and together we are stronger and can accomplish anything.

DIY, Do It Yourself. Growing up punk in the 90s, it wasn't yet mainstream. Our scene was starting to make a breakthrough with bands like Rancid, The Offspring, Bad Religion, and how could we not recognize Green Day who was getting regular radio airplay and spots on MTV. Local bands had to work, and they had to work hard. Cassettes and CDs were recorded at others' homes that had minimal equipment. Insert cards were hand made, mass copied at Kinkos, folded and stuffed by bands and friends. Getting gigs was knowing people and talking, the same as getting a crowd at the show. We'd plaster homemade flyers on every telephone pole, record shop, and run-down, smoke-filled diner we could. We made it work, and all pushed each other to keep climbing. DIY gave us a strong work ethic to rely on ourselves and our crew, and this only strengthened our unity.

These two qualities are crucial in education. I have been fortunate enough to meet another educator through Twitter, Josh Buckley, @JoshRBuckley, that shares this mentality. We started talking, shared a few phone calls, and before you know it had launched The Punk Rock Classrooms Podcast! Our creed, our mantra, is Passion x Unity x DIY. We've been expanding to be more than just a podcast, and by the time you're reading this book who knows what we'll have accomplished. We have plans for The Punk Rock Classrooms book where we'll dive deeper into the connections between the Punk Rock mindset and education. But for this book, *The EduCulture Cookbook*, we need to discuss our first tenet, Passion.

Passion. We hear it all the time, "You must bring your passion to the classroom. Share your passion with your students." I'm going to discuss those statements a little bit, but explain why passion is crucial, why it's a necessity for our schools and classrooms, and why every educator, regardless of their role, must bring their passion. I'm going to accomplish all of this by explaining the power of passion through Punk Rock. How that passion came through the speakers while I was infesting my eardrums with a beauty that took me to another place. How the passion bands displayed on stage, while playing live, ignited the venue, making every kid in the crowd not just an audience member, but an integral part of the show. How that passion, that energy that connected us all, made it an experience we would never forget. Everything that haunted us was exorcised and together we knew we could handle anything life would throw at us.

Bands have a tough job. They tour the country, playing night after night in various venues, cranking out the same songs every night to a new crowd. Think about this - bands who have been around for years, bands like NOFX, Sick of it All, and Bad Religion have been playing some tunes that are 30 years old! I've been to some shows where a fan calls out a song to be played and the band responds, "We've retired that one, we got sick of playing it."

Teachers can take a lesson from this. When lessons get old and stale, and it feels more like a chore to prepare it and bring it to your students, get rid of it. You don't need to continue to teach that lesson just because you have for the past 20 years! If your fire isn't there, move on and find something new. Now I'm not saying just because a lesson is old it's time to ditch it. I've seen Sick of It All play "It's Clobberin' Time" like it was just released. They still believe in that track that was written over 20 years ago. Sure, there's a few changes live, it's spiced up, but the content is the same. If you still believe in a lesson, and it fits with what students need to be learning in today's world, tweak it to the times.

Word gets around about bands' shows. This comes back to the unity and DIY tenets I mentioned above. Before a band would make it to our neck of the woods, someone in our crew who knew someone in a crew from Michigan would talk on the phone and let us know if we were either in for a treat, an experience we'd never forget, or if we would see a band just going through the motions. Word gets around, and no one wants to be known as the educator that goes through the motions and completes a job day in and day out. Be the one that brings your passion every day. Those are the hallway and lunchroom gossip you want about you.

Ok, so why do we need to bring this passion? How does what a punk rock band does on stage relate to schools and classrooms? The band controls the energy, the experience for the audience. I've been to shows where the band is simply just playing their songs, going through their setlist. No passion. No energy. No experience. These shows did nothing for me. I was just a member of the audience, no escape.

On the other hand, there were the bands, like the ones I mentioned above, that brought their passion every night, every year, every show. The knew, like the hardcore band Bane states, "This is for the kids!" These shows, the bands knew how much they meant to the audience, to the kids. They have either been in our shoes, or currently were, and understood the outlet and release that was needed for everyone there. They knew that it wasn't just them on stage, doing their thing, that everyone in that venue was a part of the show. They knew we needed an experience, we needed to dance, sing along, and sweat together. These bands knew that it was their obligation to bring their passion to every song played at every show, no matter how many times they already had. If it gets stale for them, it gets taken off of the setlist. These bands knew the kids don't' deserve something that they themselves do not have a belief and passion for.

Bring your passion to school every day. Our students are relying on you. They are yearning for an experience, a connection, a memory that will take them away from all of the problems they are facing. Be the teacher that gets talked about in the hallways, lunchroom, and playground. Have the show that kids are cramming through the doorway for, standing room only. Bring your excitement every day. The bands that have been doing this for 20, 30 years can do that because they haven't lost their passion and they're still making a difference in a new generation of young punks. If we don't bring our passions and excitement to our students, we will either force ourselves out of the profession or just have a miserable countdown to retirement.

By bringing your passion to the classroom you will help your students more than you know. Colleagues will feel your energy and want to be a part of the show. You will look forward to each day in the classroom, even if it's been 30 years.

POP PUNK PASSION PIZZA

INGREDIENTS

1. Have a hobby you're passionate about
2. Have no fear, but excitement to share your passion with others
3. Lesson plan book or computer program
4. A day, hopefully, more than one, where you can share your passion with staff/students

TIME

- Prep Time - 60 minutes
- Cook Time - 60 minutes
- Total Time - 2 hours
- Total Cost - $0.00

PROCEDURE

1. Acknowledge the passion you have outside of school.
2. Brainstorm various ideas & approaches to sharing your passion with staff/students.
3. Analyze your list of ideas, narrowing down to what approach you feel the most excited about!
4. Lesson plan passion project.
5. Build anticipation amongst students/staff about your upcoming passion lesson (or don't. Sometimes it's an amazing surprise to just bust out your passion activity!)
6. Implement your passion lesson.
7. Be open to answering questions & holding discussions with students/staff regarding your passion.
8. Enjoy the lesson, enjoy the day! Find more ways to bring your passion to build excitement to students/staff.

Salt
By Josh Buckley
@JoshRBuckley
@PunkClassrooms
Teacher & Co-host of Punk Rock Classrooms

Look, I'm not much of a cook, but I watch a lot of cooking shows. I'm a sucker for watching people do something they love and something I'm admittedly not great at. There is one key ingredient in almost everything I see them make whether they are baking cake or making tacos and that's salt. It always looks like way more than what I would put in but again, I'm no cook. But on every one of those shows, the cookies turn out perfect, the mashed potatoes are on point, and the salsa is excellent. It's about putting the right things into what you make.

What I do know though is teaching and that key ingredient in the classroom that we don't always put enough in but we should is PASSION. It's the easiest thing to leave out of a lesson plan, but it's that spice that gives any lesson, whether it's teaching the electoral college or the Phillips curve, the flavor it needs. Did I mention I was a social studies teacher? Anyway, that passion that we bring into the classroom is what helps us build relationships, helps us build excitement for learning, and creates a space where we can all celebrate the success of each student.

If we leave out that passion, we are leaving out that oh so necessary piece of the recipe. Mike has set up some great ways for you to connect with your staff, your students, and your community, but if you walk in that room devoid of passion, if you walk into that room and you forgot to add the "salt," you are setting yourself up for just going through the motions and never connecting. Our passion, our attitude, is contagious. I teach economics and there is a reason it is often referred to as the dismal science. But it's not the great lesson plan I put together or the interactive slideshow I made that creates a classroom environment where my kids get into drawing supply curves; it's the passion. It's the energy I walk in with. It's the excitement I have for teaching. That passion goes a long way.

Let's go back to those cooking shows for a minute. I'm gonna be honest, I'm never going to be the next baking star or the next food truck king. So why do I watch those shows? It's not just the salt they add to their ingredients; they bring passion too. And if I don't see it in the chef on the screen, I'll find the next cooking show to binge. Our students are the same way. They can easily "change the channel." So, show them you are passionate about teaching. Show them why you love teaching and even though they may not grow up not using the cost-benefit analysis tool you showed them in class, at least they knew you cared. At least they felt the excitement and joined in.

So when you bake your cookies, don't forget the salt and when you teach your next class, don't forget your passion.

Passion
By Elijah Carbajal
@carbaeli
Teacher & Blogger

I didn't do a lot right during my first year of teaching. When I think back to that year, I am embarrassed even by my own remembrances of a young kid, fresh out of college trying to manage 22 fourth graders. I yelled. A lot. I taught mediocre lessons because I was too stinking tired to push myself. Yes, I made a lot of mistakes that year, but I will say there is one thing I did right that year. It would be the first of many times to come where I would teach a skill through a passion of mine.
That year, I decided to teach the students reading and research skills by exploring social injustices and letting students brain-

storm ways to fight them. I've always been intrigued by events like the Holocaust. Sad, I know; just hear me out. I enjoy studying Holocaust history, but what I'm really fascinated with is stories of survivors or people who hid Jews from the Nazis or helped them escape. I've always liked the hero of the story. I also care about the one who is being saved. So, I don't know. I guess I'm passionate about social justice because it seems like the obvious thing to be passionate about. But I digress.

I started on Valentine's Day. Perfect day to start. "Why was it the perfect day to start this project?" I'm so glad you asked! My students didn't realize that St. Valentine was an actual person, who, according to legend, married couples to help spare husbands from war, even though he was ordered not to do so. Basically, he defied an order because he felt inside that it was wrong. He was later arrested and put to death for this. (And that's how I turned a happy Valentine's Day into a bloody Valentine's Day. Yikes!) Well, the students, believe or not, found it interesting. We began exploring other social problems: racism, bullying, homelessness, poverty, littering, and more topics that came up. Each student selected a topic to explore. Some students teamed up. Every student did research. Some even researched surveys at the school administered by them!

What happened? The Passion ignited a flame, which ignited another flame, and another, and another. Teachers, when you bring your passion to school, you draw out the passion of students. I didn't know the little girl in my class, holding a mirror out and telling everyone to see how beautiful they are, was so passionate about helping others. (Future activist?) Passion leads us to new places. Here are some.

Engagement. Teaching skills through your passion is what engages students. They are engaged even more when skills are taught through the things they are passionate about. Teaching about fractions? Ask them to shoot hoops, bump a volleyball, kick a soccer ball, etc. and show their results in a fraction. What about music? Teach poetry through songs. Let them suggest songs to analyze, lyrically and musically, making connections about how the music and the lyrics match. Art? Don't give them a worksheet about Michelangelo. Let them paint a picture taped to the bottom of the desk while they lay on their backs. Add some passion, and your kids will engage themselves! Authentic learning was taking place in my classroom. (Maybe that year *wasn't* as bad as I thought it was.)

It leads to discovery. One man's treasure can also be another person's treasure. I play bass guitar and guitar. I can remember, as a little kid, watching old videos of gospel music, imitating the guitar players, or playing air guitar in the van on the way to church. I was, admittedly, a headphone singer when I was little, and I sang loudly and very off-key. Music has always been a part of my life because of the passion that my parents, especially my dad, have for music. They exposed me to music, which sparked joy and passion for music that has stuck with me ever since. You just never know what your kids will discover about themselves until you bring your passion to the classroom.

Passion leads to student voice and choice. Not every kid in my class reported their findings in the same way. Some gave demonstrations, like the girl with the mirror I mentioned earlier. Some created bar graphs to show the number of students who were bullied and in what form. Other students created PowerPoint Presentations on their hobbies and interests. When you introduce passion into your classrooms, the door leading to expression opens. Some of our students are okay writing essays, and others want to create a video. Some teachers let their kids podcast, and other teachers let their kids blog. One isn't better than the other; both are awesome ways for students to express their learning. Let our passion and the passion of our students free us to teach, learn, and express our learning in ways that reflect who we are.

It is my hope that you can find a way to bring your passion into the classroom. How can you use crocheting in your math class? How can you use yoga to teach social-emotional skills? How many demonstrations could you do with shark teeth? Can you use jump roping to explore poetry? Get creative. To be creative just start with a simple question: how can my passion and the passion of my students be used to help us understand this skill/concept? As the idea comes, try it out. Don't let fear keep you from trying something new that just might change a student's life.

14

RED VELVET VIDEO VLOGS

It was a typical mid-morning Tuesday. I was loving the day, skateboarding from classroom to classroom, checking in on staff and the awesome mind-expanding activities our kids were engrossed in. I rolled past a fourth-grade classroom, saw kids up, talking, collaborating, and I planned on popping in on my way back down the hall to see what they were up to.

"Hey Mr. Earnshaw, you want to try some sushi?"

I quickly pulled a powerslide on my skateboard, intrigued, yet frightened. I popped my board up by kicking my right Van sneaker on the tail of my board, catching it by the trucks briefly after it launched off of the solid ground. I briskly headed back to the room on foot.

"Huh, did you say sushi? I'm not a fan of seafood at all, you are?" I asked 28 fourth graders. I was already floored that kids were ingesting sushi in a classroom, but it was their collective response that had me flabbergasted!

"YES! It's sooooo good! You need to try one!" was shouted at me from multiple corners of the room. I was caught in the middle of the surround sound of ten- and eleven-year-olds praising their love of sushi.

My eyes bugged, nose shriveled, and I muttered, "Uuummm, no way! Seafood is not my thing!"

The chants began, them against me, "C'mon...Try It...Try It...Try It..."

Just as I dropped my board to the floor, looking for a clean, quick, escape route, their teacher chimed in. "Hey, Megan, Kara, and Becky, why don't you show Mr. Earnshaw how you make sushi."

I was at a turning point at this time of the year. We had just completed our state testing, formal evaluation season was over, and the Spring weather was beginning to break through that thin wall of ice. Our staff had done a phenomenal job up to this point on sharing our voices, collaborating, and working together to change the lives of our kids. **Schools aren't built for us, to have jobs. Schools are here for the kids, to give them a better life. Schools are here for us to empower students to build confidence in themselves and their strengths, for students to know where they have areas to grow, to understand the power of collaboration to solve problems, and to leave our schools determined to change the world.** We were getting there, but we needed to step it up. We needed to find a way to give students an outlet of their own to share their voice.

The girls were about to explain how to prepare sushi; they were going to swim me through the process right there in the classroom. It was at that moment, I could see the words about to escape their mouths, and I stopped them before they could fill the air and meet my ears.

"Wait, don't tell me now. How would you like to teach me how to make sushi on video and we'll post it to our YouTube channel?"

These were fourth graders, so I'm pretty positive you know what their response was.

Before we could just record a video with students and post to YouTube, which would then be shared on our other various social media accounts, we needed some permission. This is where teamwork comes in between the teacher and admin. I have access to student demographics and the phone numbers parents registered with, but those only get one so far. I was excited. I was ready to get this new chapter in our school's culture started, and I was so stoked that it would be in the hands of our students; they would be the stars! The kids were more excited than I was, and I knew we needed to make this video today while the grill was hot (even though sushi is raw).

"Mike, I can just Remind message the parents and ask for permission. They respond pretty quick when it's a text," their teacher, my comrade in this process, said.

"Perfect!" I replied. "Girls, as soon as we have permission from your parents, we'll shoot the video. Cool?"

The students all agreed that it would work, but they still had one question for me. "So, Mr. Earnshaw, are you going to eat the sushi after we make it?"

I took a big gulp, not the oversized soda you buy from 7-11, but a big gulp in my throat at the thought of raw fish entering my stomach.

The permission didn't take long at all. I had skated up to the front office to have lunch with our office staff. Before the beeping on the microwave could infiltrate the air, I had a message that all of the girls' parents had consented to filming of the video. I was excited about this, as we were about to turn a new corner with student voice in our school, but then I quickly remembered I'd be eating sushi. As my stomach was already churning, I forced down the leftover tacos just to have something other than raw fish eggs in me.

"All right, so basically I will do the welcome, state who I am, the name of our show (which we decided would be called, "Sharing Smarts with the OG Grizzlies"), and then introduce the three of you. We'll then state why we're here, what you're going to show us, and how it relates to what you were learning in class."

The girls did a phenomenal job! We were able to get the short segment recorded in one take! I stated the intro which consisted of announcing what our show was, who I was, then having the girls introduce themselves, and what they were going to be teaching me. Which, in case you forgot, was how to make sushi, and, if you forgot, I am deathly afraid to eat.

Sweat began to grow on my brow like crabgrass during a summer drought. Palms were sweaty. A nervous smile and chuckle became my defense as I knew I was going to have to consume the sushi these amazing students were making for me. Only, I didn't know if I would be able to stomach it. I honestly cannot consume seafood. I believe it stems from working as a head cook for nearly 10 years and the smell of fish going bad never left my nasal cavity. I just cannot eat anything from the waters.

The girls were up, here we go!

"First, you take a Rice Krispy treat and flatten it down with your hand. You want to get it thin and flexible without breaking."

I chimed in, "And of course make sure your hands are washed before preparing any meal, especially this sushi recipe!" This gave all the girls a laugh and they assured me, and the audience, that their teacher had them wash their hands before heading to our broadcasting studio.

"Next, you place a Swedish Fish in the center of your flattened out Rice Krispy treat."

"Finally, roll up the Rice Krispy treat from one end to the next."

"Oh wait! There's one more step, wrap a Fruit By The Foot around the rolled-up Rice Krispy treat! Are you ready to eat it, Mr. Earnshaw?"

Now all eyes were on me, the three girls sharing how to make sushi on our first recorded student-led vlog, and all those that were going to be watching this. This was time to not let them down. I could've taken a small bite and forced its travels down my throat and into my stomach. Instead, I took a bite that removed half of the sushi into my gullet! I chewed, smiled at the camera, and declared, "This is the best sushi I've ever had!"

It was true, that was not only the first time I've eaten sushi, but it was delicious!

After I fulfilled my promise to these students and tried their sushi, which I finished, the girls spent time talking about why they were making this delicious delicacy in their class. They talked about a story they read together, about a girl from Japan who moved to the United States and was longing to share traditions from her family and homeland. The girls then discussed why we need to learn about others and accept our differences. They discussed how we all have strengths and qualities that others may not have, and we must share them and rely on others where we have areas to grow. The girls discussed why we need to work together to make our school, community, and world a better place.

The conversation the girls had about empathy, acceptance, and working towards change is what this is all about. This conversation gave me hope that our future was in great hands. It also assured me that our teachers knew the impact and importance of providing lessons that were hands-on, outside of the box, fun and engaging, all the while teaching to state standards and life skills that our kids need to change our world.

This crucial conversation, with three fourth grade girls, about changing our world for the better, proves that my mission, our mission, is being worked towards. And none of this would have happened if it wasn't for a teacher deciding to take a story of empathy and creating an activity where kids made candy sushi which was shared for the world to see.

Find ways for students to speak, to share, to take ownership. Our kids' entire lives have been spent being able to watch what they want when they want. YouTube, TikTok, Google, all of these amazing and reliable apps are our students' world; it is ingrained into their lives. Having students share a fun activity on camera, something they long for, teaches so much. As mentioned above, we can assess them on what they know related to the lesson and curriculum. We also get to teach them. We teach them about how what is put on video and placed on the internet is for everyone to see. We teach them that we must present ourselves as we want others to see us. We teach students how to positively represent our school, our families, and ourselves. We get to teach students how to record, edit, publish, and promote their work. These are all skills that will carry them far in life, skills I wish I had acquired when I was their age.

Find ways to let students share their voices. They will not be the only ones that learn something to improve their life.

RED VELVET VIDEO VLOGS

INGREDIENTS

1. Have a hobby you're passionate about
2. Have no fear, but excitement to share your passion with others
3. Lesson plan book or computer program
4. A day, hopefully, more than one, where you can share your passion with staff/students

TIME

- Prep Time - 60 minutes
- Cook Time - 60 minutes
- Total Time - 2 hours
- Total Cost - $0.00

PROCEDURE

1. Acknowledge the passion you have outside of school.
2. Brainstorm various ideas & approaches to sharing your passion with staff/students.
3. Analyze your list of ideas, narrowing down to what approach you feel the most excited about!
4. Lesson plan passion project.
5. Build anticipation amongst students/staff about your upcoming passion lesson (or don't. Sometimes it's an amazing surprise to just bust out your passion activity!)
6. Implement your passion lesson.
7. Be open to answering questions & holding discussions with students/staff regarding your passion.
8. Enjoy the lesson, enjoy the day! Find more ways to bring your passion to build excitement to students/staff.

How Video Can Enhance Student Voice and Culture
By Christine Ravesi-Weinstein, M. Ed
@RavesiWeinstein
Assistant Principal

I started my journey of mental health advocacy in June of 2017 when I co-founded a non-profit organization: *Running from Anxiety*. The work of the organization was centered around personal experience; movement, and the endorphins released along with it, reduces the feelings of anxiety in an otherwise anxious mind. We worked raising money to provide a yearly scholarship for a graduating senior who dealt with mental illness during their lifetime. We also organized community runs, support group meetings, and a 5K race. The work I was doing brought me much joy, but after two years, was not reaching a wide enough audience.

In March of 2019, I started writing. The pieces I authored were blogs that spoke to my experience, but in an academic way. Through my writing, I sought to provide readers with strategies and advice for working with students suffering from anxiety. The blogs I wrote were impactful. Many were published in *eSchoolNews*, the *Teach Better Team Blog*, and *District Administration*. People began following me on social media, and my name was starting to become commonplace in the world of mental health advocacy.

But there was a big piece of me that was missing from all the articles I wrote. While I felt that my expertise and experience were able to shine in my publications, I didn't feel like my truth, my own anxiety, and my authenticity really could.

I ventured into the world of video in the spring and early summer of the same year. As a recreational photographer for years, being behind the camera felt like a second home; being in

front of it, however, was terrifying. I had no idea what to say, or w
here, or even how to say it.

"What do you think about while you're running?" A friend of mine asked.

"I don't know," I replied. "How much I hate it, I guess."
The idea for the video was born from that friend's question. I started filming one to two-minute videos after a run or workout. I focused on explaining to viewers what I was thinking about while exercising, being sure to connect it to the anxious students in their classrooms.

The use of video provided me with the voice that the written word could not. It allowed me to be more vulnerable, more authentic, and a better advocate; I was able to show viewers what anxiety actually looked like rather than task them with creating a mental picture on their own.

Video became the foundation of my work as a mental health advocate. It gave me an even greater following on social media, drawing attention to the publications I had worked on previously. I was able to connect with the audience. They could see my demeanor, feel my words, and see my eyes. Video allowed the audience to trust me. Sure, expertise can be shown in a CV, but expertise can be felt in a video.

My use of video gave me a voice for mental health advocacy on which I wanted to expand. I decided to pair my writing with my new love of video, and produce my own vlog, i.e., video blog. Using only an iPhone and a few apps, I began producing "Vlogging with Anxiety." Viewers could now "read" my strategies while simultaneously feeling my experiences. It was a match made in heaven.

Video isn't just a tool; it's a culture. It allows a voice to be heard through the use of creativity and expertise. Allowing students to use video as a platform through which we assess their proficiency on state and local standards is a game-changer, a culture shift. Video teaches so many invaluable lessons to students: creativity, vulnerability, writing (if a script is required), editing, communication, collaboration, performance, handling adversity, and production, just to name a few. No other assignment or task we ask students to engage in is going to check off more, or even an equivalent number of, boxes.

In my experience as an educator, video gives students a voice, just as it has for me. If we implement it correctly, it can even change the culture of teaching and learning in our buildings. Video can become the foundation of communication between students and teachers as well as administration and faculty. It can provide students with confidence emotionally and academically. Video is a voice for students unlike any other platform in the world of academia. It is our responsibility as educators to provide students with the opportunity to engage with it.

15

SUMMER SELFIE SANGRIA

Have you ever felt like you were the only one not sharing in the joy and happiness that everyone around you was? It's like, you're at that local summer BBQ, and Karen from the end of the block made a killer sangria. Everyone has their red Solo cup topped off, filling the air with laughter after each lame "parent" joke. Inhibitions are lowered just a little, and it is only 3:30 in the afternoon. You grab a cup for yourself, there's plenty left on the table, and then you skedaddle over to the beverage table where everyone has gotten the good stuff. Only you are left to find an empty pitcher, the insides stained a purple-ish-red, some fruit left to be discarded resting on the bottom floor. You glance over your left shoulder to glare at that one most close to you, that significant other, only to see them with a full cup, placing their hand on their BFF's shoulder for balance as they laugh hysterically, tears escaping their eyes, at the story they've heard every BBQ for the past 7 years.

We've all been there. Maybe not like the scenario mentioned above, but we've all experienced the feeling of being the only one not sharing joy, happiness, and excitement. This happened for me during May 2019. Staff was looking forward to vacations, time with their families, parties, BBQs, and a much-needed break from the hard, heart-wrenching work we do as educators. I'm not faulting our amazing staff, or any educator, for looking forward to nearly three months of a vacation. They have earned it, and I want nothing more for them to enjoy this time they have earned. Teaching is hard work; it is a 12-month job that only teachers and paraprofessionals get done in about 9.

Ever since I have become an administrator, I've had a 12-month contract. I'm not complaining. There is a ton of behind the scenes work principals and assistant principals need to complete during those summer months when the classrooms and halls are empty. Let's be honest, we're not even working full shifts. Typically, Fridays are off, hours are flexible, and it's easy to space out what needs to get done. Why was I upset then? Why was I sad, shedding a tear or two, that I wasn't getting a cup of Sangria like our staff? That's because we were just coming off of one of the best positive culture building school years ever! Our staff had come leaps and bounds collaboratively this past year. Staff had put relationships first and saw the world-changing effects that they could make in the lives of our students. I was saddened because I feared that all of the progress we made would be lost through the same Summer Slump they say students face, and the following school year we would be staring back at Ground Zero. I needed something to stay connected to our staff, something to keep the culture-building going strong. **School culture isn't one and done. School culture is ongoing; we need to keep putting logs into the fire.** I needed a culture-building activity that wouldn't get me a grievance by going against the staff's contract and asking them to work during their time off.

I can't stress enough how benefitting it is to be a connected educator. My preference is Twitter, but there are so many other social media sites and groups to join. Educators need to know what is going on in the world of education outside of their classrooms, school walls, and district boundaries. There are amazing, world-changing activities and approaches to impacting the lives of our kids happening all across the country that we would be doing our students a disservice by not connecting and opening our eyes to what others are doing. And it goes vice versa; we need to share what we are doing. **Education is not a place to have egos and keep activities and approaches to ourselves. Education is about changing the lives of our students for the better, empowering them to leave our buildings determined to change the world.** That is not going to happen if we only look to ourselves to teach them.

I came across a Tweet from a good friend of mine, Matt Arend, that I had met through using #Fitleaders. Matt and I are both distance runners. We're also principals, and after getting involved in Voxer realized we were both members of the #PrincipalsinAction group. Matt had just accepted a new principalship position and shared his excitement through Twitter. I came across a tweet one night where Matt mentioned something he was doing over the summer months to connect with his new staff, Summer Selfie Bingo.

I was intrigued. I needed to know more. Summer Selfie Bingo sounded like the perfect recipe to cook up for some positive culture building during those summer months that I was apart from our staff. I needed to know more about it. Luckily, Matt Arend is the type of educator that shares the amazing things he does with his staff, students, and parents. Matt knows that what works isn't to be kept a secret as it can benefit so many more. I was grateful to find that Matt's Summer Selfie Bingo Recipe had a link to a Google Doc of the Bingo Board in his Tweet.

My eyes grazed Matt's Google Doc that included a Summer Selfie Bingo Board for approximately 2.7 seconds and I knew this was the perfect recipe for staying connected through summer. I was going to follow what Matt lined out. It was already pretty damn near perfect, but I saw some opportunities to add a few more spices of my own. As always, no recipe is ever followed to the T.

I was so excited to know that there was a way for us to continue the strong bonds we welded together the past year. I didn't want to look too overzealous, so I just threw the topic in a weekly FYI email. I wanted to garner some interest from the staff, build the anticipation, let the aroma from the dish waft from the kitchen into the dining room. I dropped a line something like this.

"The year is coming to an end, but we don't have to let the fun stop! Our first annual Summer Selfie Bingo challenge will be happening! Sign up at the following link to play. More info to come!"

That was it. I cracked the door to my kitchen about three weeks before the year ended, just enough time to get our staff talking and excited. Each week that passed, I mentioned it, in just as much detail as the first time. Everyone I had a one-on-one conversation with I found a way to bring it up, sharing my excitement and enthusiasm, trying to get as many participants as I could.

The summer began and we had more Bingo players than I could have hoped for! We had players that I had never would've thought wanted to play! The game started out simple. I created a mass group on WhatsApp for everyone that was in. I shared out the Bingo Board. It was made up of fun topics, Starbucks Selfie, Beach Selfie, Food Truck Selfie, etc. Lots of topics that anyone that spends time traveling, vacationing, or making memories with families will encounter. The rules were simple; everyone could submit one selfie to our group app per day. This would help to have the game last longer than the first few weeks of summer.

Summer Selfie Bingo was just what we needed to remain connected, have a good time, and learn about one another's lives outside of our school year. Of course, people were creative, finding ways to make the topic pics fun. But the best part was that everyone started making up their own topics and selfie pics! Off the wall pics were coming through, like "Stalker Selfie" when our Assistant Principal went for a bike ride with her daughter past the house I had just moved into!

One night, during a family trip to Target (I know, I live a wild and crazy life), I ran into one of our kindergarten teachers. What did we do? We took a "Target Selfie." I sent it out to the group stating "Bonus Points!" It got a good, friendly, fire going with the group. Then, I couldn't have planned it any better. I ran into one of our fourth-grade teachers the very next day…AT THE BEACH! Yep, Bonus Points!

There were no prizes to be given, no true winner at the end of the summer. This game was about educators, colleagues, individuals, connecting outside of the workday. We learned about each other, our hobbies, likes/dislikes, traditions, quirks, and most importantly, our families. Did any of this have anything to do with improving and changing the lives of our students? You bet it did! By having us connect on a fun, human level, when we returned for the next school year we had a bond. We had inside jokes and stories that were told through really bad selfies that weren't photoshopped. We knew, because of a picture of one of us eating an ice cream cone or drinking alcoholic seltzer water on the beach, that we had each other's backs. Whatever this upcoming year would throw at us, we would get through it together, regardless of grade assignment, title, or role. We were a family and would do whatever it took to better our students.

The next year was one we needed these bonds more than ever. We were about to enter the 2019/2020 School Year known as #COVID19.

SUMMER SELFIE SANGRIA

INGREDIENTS

1. Weekly newsletter or group/staff email
2. Cell phone w/ a camera & internet access
3. Downloadable large group sharing app
4. Group/staff phone numbers
5. Creativity

TIME

- Prep Time - 3 weeks
- Cook Time - 2.5 months
- Total Time - 3.1 months
- Total Cost - The cost of a text if your cell carrier charges

PROCEDURE

1. Send out an email to get interest in playing Summer Selfie Bingo.
2. Create a form to track those that express an interest to play.
3. Set a start & end date for Summer Selfie Bingo.
4. Create & enter all participants into the large group sharing app.
5. Share the Summer Selfie Bingo Board w/ participants the morning of the first day.
6. Take 1 selfie per day & share with the group.
7. Take selfies that cover the board categories & those that do not! Be creative & have fun!

Selfies!
By Kim Nye
4th Grade Teacher

Mike prides himself on building a family-like atmosphere at our school. He constantly provides activities for the staff to involve themselves in to aid in this culture. For instance, one summer he decided to hold a Summer Bingo. This wasn't a requirement, but a great way to not only get involved during our time off, but to also learn about one another. The game consisted of everyone downloading a specific app and uploading pictures of ourselves or family doing activities.

One summer day, I took my daughters to the beach. Not long after relaxing and catching some rays, I ran into Mike and his family. We were able to take a picture together and cross off a Bingo square. I do know he had run into several others during his summer break. This is a prime example of how a fun activity during teacher's time off can build culture within a school.

Building School Culture
By Matthew Arend
@matthew_arend
Principal

Building school culture is something I am passionate about and have been focused on since I walked into the door at Sigler Elementary six years ago. Author Baruti Kafele, in his book *Closing the Attitude Gap* (2013), reduces culture into one word: *lifestyle*. I want to love the *lifestyle* we cultivate and I want the amazing teachers who work here to love it too. I want folks who walk into our building to recognize the culture (*lifestyle*) we have created.

Building school culture does not just happen while school is in session. While led by the principal, developing a *lifestyle* within the walls of a classroom and school is a collective group effort, including the students, staff, teachers and community. Building school culture happens all year long. Yes, building school culture even takes place over the summer.

Yes, summer is meant to relax, unplug, reflect and recharge, but while you are doing all of those important things, do not forget you are also building school culture. You have a *lifestyle* to create in your building. What are you waiting for?

ACKNOWLEDGMENTS

I am going to do my best to acknowledge everyone that has had a part in getting me to where I am both professionally and personally. Like every award show, I'm sure I'll leave someone out. If it's you, know I'm already sorry, we'll go out for a cup of coffee or beer, my treat.

Megan, Evan, and Aubrey. You have no idea how deep my love for all of you is. I know I don't always show it and am very selfish with what I want in life. I promise to work on that. I can't thank you enough for always supporting me and my passions. Your support is all I need to keep going. I love you more than any words I could ever write. Please know that I will always support you as you have for me.

To my family and friends, thank you for all of the laughs we share together. You have no idea how much I look forward to every party, bbq, pool volleyball game, or anytime we make an excuse to get together and celebrate. You all help to keep me sane and refreshed when the stress of "the job" gets so overwhelming. I look forward to many more memories together and more chances to prove myself at volleyball and why I should be a First Round Pick.

Mom and Dad, thank you for allowing me to follow my passions, blast punk rock throughout our house walls, ride a skateboard, and express myself how I wanted to throughout my youth. This has helped to instill upon me the power of staying true to ourselves, embracing differences, and uniting together to build upon each other's strengths.

Josh Buckley, my brother-in-arms. Crazy to think we've never met in person. I feel like I've known you forever! Thank you for taking a chance on me and venturing down the Punk Rock Classrooms road together. I know that we've barely Scratched the Surface. We're going to change the way educators approach teaching, and I wouldn't want to be on that mission with anyone else.

Jeff Kubiak, your friendship has meant more to me than you know. We have shared so many deep, emotional conversations about all aspects of life. From when we first met in Ohio in November 2019, I knew that I had a great friend. You push me, you challenge me, and you are always there for me. I can't thank you enough. I only hope that I am able to be there for you as you are for me.

Kristen Nann. Honestly, we may not be reading this book right now if it wasn't for you attending my session at Teach Better 19 and laughing throughout most of my presentation! At first, I thought I was that bad, but afterwards you assured me that it was just my authentic story-telling that you connected with. Thank you for your belief and support of me.

Sarah Thomas, Mandy Froehlich, and the entire EduMatch Family! Thank you so much for taking the chance and believing in a punk rock loving, skateboarding, principal extraordinaire! I have felt at home since our first conversation when my dream was only a few chapters. Your acceptance, belief, & excitement for my passion project mean the world to me and I am so glad we're running in the same crew.

To the staff at Oak Glen Elementary School. Years ago you welcomed me in as a first-year principal. You've seen my ups and downs, called me out on mistakes, and worked with me to become the effective leader you deserve. We've been through a lot together, and the fact that you have trusted me enough to lead true to who I am and do things the way I know education needs to be done means the world.

ABOUT THE AUTHOR

First and foremost, Michael Earnshaw is a father to two beautiful children, husband to the most amazing woman in the universe, and Dog Dad to the one and only goldendoodle, Ruby Mae. He spent nearly fifteen years as a middle-school ELA teacher before transitioning into school administration.

Michael believes that in order to empower students and staff to know their strengths, own their areas of growth, be comfortable with collaboration, and confident in the power of their voice to change this world for the better, it all begins with trusting relationships and a positive school culture. Michael's approaches are hands-on, out of the box, and fun, all while fostering growth and learning.

Michael loves to share his vision and approaches to education through speaking at educational conferences, blogging, writing, and talking on his podcast, Punk Rock Classrooms.

When Michael is not trying to make the world a better place, spreading his message, and spending time with his family you can find him training for marathons with early morning runs, pretending he's strong in his basement gym, and listening to punk rock and skateboarding.

Here's how to connect with Michael Earnshaw or invite him to your next conference or professional development session:

Twitter:

@MikeREarnshaw

@PunkClassrooms

Email:

EduCultureCookbook@yahoo.com

REFERENCES

Kamb, S. (2019, August 12). Iron and the Soul - Henry Rollins. Retrieved September 30, 2020, from https://www.nerdfitness.com/blog/iron-and-the-soul/

Kafele, B. K. (2013). *Closing the attitude gap: How to fire up your students to strive for success.* Alexandria, Virginia USA, VA: ASCD.

www.ingramcontent.com/pod-product-compliance
Lightning Source LLC
Chambersburg PA
CBHW071415070526
44578CB00003B/581